Memoirs of a Reluctant Servant

Two years of Triumph and Sorrow in Liberia, Africa

By: JEROME CABEEN

With Barbara Pawlikowski

Order this book online at www.trafford.com
or email orders@trafford.com

Most Trafford titles are also available at major online book retailers.

Printed in the United States of America.

ISBN: 978-1-4251-5273-4 (sc)
ISBN: 978-1-4269-6575-3 (hc)
ISBN: 978-1-4269-6607-1 (e)

Library of Congress Control Number: 2011906122

Trafford rev. 05/02/2011

 www.trafford.com

North America & international
toll-free: 1 888 232 4444 (USA & Canada)
phone: 250 383 6864 ♦ fax: 812 355 4082

Dedication

For those still dwelling on the threshold:

My mother Joan Cabeen – Who taught me how to pray

My friend John Henry Lyons – Who taught me to love who I am

My inspiration Musu – Who taught me about forgiveness

&

My wife, companion and hero Clarisa Chavarria Lara – Who taught me about courage

For those who have crossed over the threshold and now dwell in perfect peace:

Elijah Koko (1999-2009) – I miss you more than words can express

Peter Fiah "Double D" (1988-2010) – It's your turn to laugh at us

Liberia,
Africa

Atlantic
Ocean

Prologue

It had to be God who called me to Africa. I was more than content to stay in Honduras serving the children I had come to know and love so dearly. You might call me a reluctant servant when it comes to Africa, though it did intrigue me. I was born in Texas but Honduras had been my home for the last four years and I came to love the country so much that in 2007 I had a beautiful tattoo of the Central American republic emblazoned on my back.

It wasn't necessarily my idea to leave my newly adopted country. My wife, Clarisa, a native Honduran, had a genuine desire to do missionary work on the African continent, and so in an attempt to please both God and my wife, I once again uprooted myself and traveled to a place I'd only read about; this time, Liberia. The country was still recovering from its second brutal civil war — near constant conflicts that lasted over 20 years. As a result, Liberia had been listed by many of the world's leading NGOs and periodicals as the worst and most violent place in the world to live.

I've been around too long and seen too many bad things to walk into a situation naively. Even so, that didn't mean I was prepared for what was to come.

We were on our final approach to the runway at Roberts International Airport just outside of Monrovia when the question, "Where are we?" hit me. I thought we were supposed to land in the largest city in Liberia, but I felt like we'd arrived at the end of the earth instead. Nothing outside the window said we were anywhere near civilization. All that greeted my eyes was the pitch black darkness of the African sky above.

In contrast, an hour earlier, just as dusk was waving the white flag of surrender to nightfall, Clarisa and I had landed in Abidjan, the Ivory Coast. Now that is a city. As we descended through the cloudless sky we were greeted by a spectacle of color, rhythm and movement as the lights of Abidjan sprawled across the landscape as far as the eye could see. Even from my window seat thousands of feet above, I could feel the city's pulsating vibe. I knew that somewhere below me would be a dingy, poorly lit jazz café with an old black man banging out Thelonius Monk on a slightly out of tune piano; his cigarette smoke ascending in slowly moving coils towards the ceiling fan.

I was jealous.

But now, nothing. No lights. No vibe. No life greeted us as the big 757's tires grabbed the runway and came to a hurried stop in front of the small building that served as the airport's sole terminal. Granted, Liberia had barely emerged from a second devastating civil war just five years previous, but my first thought upon landing was that Charles Taylor, despot of despots, had somehow destroyed every single thing in the country. As we descended the portable stairs to the tarmac below, the infamous heat and humidity I had heard so much about greeted us with a stifling embrace.

I felt like Neil Armstrong landing on the face of the moon. I turned to Clarisa, "Welcome to the end of the Earth, next stop oblivion," I quipped.

Then we stepped through the doors of the terminal and into a welcoming blast of cold air.

Through quickly fogging glasses I saw a large sign promoting the FIFA World Cup Soccer Tournament of 2010, which would be taking place in South Africa two years hence. I immediately thought of Honduras' National Soccer Team that was about to begin a grueling ten game drive, which would last over a year; all in hopes of qualifying for just their second ever World Cup appearance. Of the many things I fell in love with in Honduras, one was soccer, a sport I had only considered a good cure for insomnia before my arrival in Central America. I quickly realized the beauty and grace that the game offered and became a huge fan of the Olimpia Lions from Tegucigalpa as well as the beloved Bi-Color, the national team that represented Honduras in international competitions.

Like the Bi-Color, Clarisa and I were about to start our own grueling journey. It would turn out to be more challenging than we ever imagined and with stakes much higher than a trip to the World Cup.

I took a deep breath as I arrived at the window where a young man stamped my passport and said to no one in particular, "Welcome to Liberia."

I smiled at Clarisa through a weary bravado that no doubt betrayed my uncertainty. We were on our way to becoming part of the great Liberian story.

Little Generals

"Then David put his hand into his bag and retrieved a stone.
He set the stone into his sling and hurled it at Goliath, the
mighty Philistine. The stone, which came from the hands of a
child, embedded itself into the brow of the giant, prostrating
him on the ground. David ran and stood over his victim and
using the giant's own sword dispatched him and then cut off
his head."
— 1 Samuel 17: 49-51

I was trying to fall back to sleep when I was jolted awake by the fetid smell of the open sewage canal on Randall Street in downtown Monrovia. Although mid-morning was rapidly approaching, I had been struggling with the desire to grab a few more winks as our white Toyota Hilux pulled into a narrow parking space in front of the Stop and Shop Grocery Store. The music of Senegalese artist Baba Maal, which had kept me in a dreamlike state for the hour and a half drive from the mission, now faded as though the rank stench somehow affected even our MP3 player.

Instinctively I hopped out of the truck and took a few small retreating steps toward the middle of the street, more willing to compete with the oncoming traffic than the odor rising from the open sewer. I inhaled deeply, but the thick congesting humidity caught in my lungs denying me of the air I had hoped for. I took in another deep breath and exhaled slowly.

Turning quickly toward the store, I noticed a figure on my periphery, "Hey my man, white man, my good friend I beg you please hear me-o."

The plea was rapid and obviously practiced, sounding as if it was the thousandth time the young man had used this introduction. I turned to face him as I reached the bed of the pickup.

He continued his rap as he quickly approached the Toyota, "Yes my good friend I am trying to get back to Grand Bassa County. As you can see I have my soap maker's certificate and I also am a certified candle maker. I just need twenty five U.S. dollars to return to my family so I can find work."

His blood-shot eyes were searching me for the slightest hint of response. The young man was no more than twenty-five years old. But his face said he had lived a hundred lifetimes and had bitterly mourned every one of them. He was adorned in a fading Detroit Pistons jersey with the number 33 emblazoned on the front. The last 3 dangled loosely as it had lost most of its thread and I was quite sure he would be left with only one 3 by day's end. Having spent eleven years of my life engrossed in the world of Houston high school and college basketball and having several friends who had played in the NBA, I didn't need to see the name on the back of the jersey to know it was an old Grant Hill model.

He peered at me somewhat puzzled when I joked that if his 3 did indeed fall off he would have to change the name on the back of his jersey from Hill to Wallace. Hill had been traded to the Orlando Magic in 2000 for Ben Wallace. Upon his arrival in Detroit, Wallace donned a number 3 jersey.

Although ridiculously hot for mid-morning, perched atop of his head was a woolen black knit cap with the Blue Devil of Duke University smiling back at me. Completing his ensemble were a pair of dark sunglasses pulled up on top of the hat. His face was youthful but pockmarked. Though still early in the day, the young man's lean frame already glistened with sweat. His sinewy arms sported a musculature that would make most defensive backs in the NFL envious. From the waist up the young man was quite a physical specimen. But below the waist was only ruin.

He wore a filthy pair of khaki cargo shorts impregnated with a lingering tang of urine. A pair of sturdy but rusting crutches was tucked underneath both arms as he balanced himself on his left leg. A shower slipper covered his left foot; like his number 3 it looked as if it could blow at any moment. I could see pavement where a right leg should have been. His entire limb was gone from just below the hip, cargo shorts tied tightly to conceal the stump.

A moment later another young man appeared, and then another and a few seconds later yet another. I was baffled at their ability to apparently materialize from out of thin air. These guys were beyond covert, they were numinous. In a matter of maybe ten seconds "Grant Hill" and I went from two to six. I looked around at the five young men standing in a semi-circle around me and envisioned what might have been if I was still coaching basketball. I had my starting five.

All of these young men sported the trappings of the United States. One wore a very nice road jersey of my own hometown NBA team, the Houston Rockets. Yao Ming had made it to Liberia. Another had on a ragged grey Tennessee Volunteers football t-shirt. Another sported an Oakland A's baseball cap and a "Ronald Gives Blood, So Should You" t-shirt displaying the familiar golden arches of McDonalds. The last of our arrivals wore a 2003 Kenny Chesney tour shirt. I couldn't help but laugh. I enquired about the shirt and he shrugged and told me a man from the U.S. Embassy gave it to him one day when he asked for money. I asked him if he knew who Kenney Chesney was.

Without missing a beat he said, "Of course I do, he's my father, and he owes me $50 dollars, and that's U.S. not Liberian."

The roar of laughter that erupted was so spontaneous and real it was as though the men surrounding me now had never seen a bad day in their lives, but I knew better. I had tears coming from my eyes I was laughing so hard. Any inhibitions I had about being in the presence of these young men were vaporized by the joke.

Besides their U.S styled apparel they all had something else in common, each one was missing a leg. When "Kenny Chesney Jr." raised his left hand to scratch his overgrown and patchy beard I noticed he was also missing his ring and pinky fingers. My desire to shop was supplanted by the stronger desire to continue my dialogue these young men.

Downtown Monrovia is inundated with hundreds of men just like the five who now stood in front of me; all of them displaced and homeless ex-soldiers who fought in the second civil war. Some had been government soldiers fighting for Charles Taylor and some had fought with one of the rebel factions that had risen up in defiance of the Taylor regime. Now, with the war over, they were all united in one common cause, survival.

It was clear to me that they had been child soldiers and I needed to hear their stories. I introduced myself, telling them my name was Jerome.

It didn't surprise me in the least when the young man in the Oakland A's cap chimed in, "Jerome? My good friend, that ain't no name for a white man!" in his thickly accented English.

I had heard this a million times before from friends in the United States, especially during my days at James Madison High School in Houston, which was 94 percent African-American when I graduated in 1985. The men started introducing themselves in rapid fire fashion. Grant Hill introduced himself as Double D, the young man in the Tennessee Volunteers shirt was Captain Crazy. Little General wore the Oakland A's cap, Original Rude Boy sported the Houston Rockets jersey, and Kenney Chesney Jr. introduced himself as Tough Trigger Master. Their nicknames reminded me of a gangsta' rap group from Compton, California. I never thought to ask their real names.

What each offered to me I accepted without question or hesitation. I listened intently as one interrupted the other trying to get as much of their stories out as they could. It was apparent that they wanted somebody to talk to and that the majority of the people they approached disregarded them as less than human. To me they were children of God; as such I saw them as my brothers. Each had a part of his life stolen by a catastrophic war and it was obvious Liberia had not been good to them, before or now. They had been caught up as children in events so far beyond their control and now those events haunted them, relegating them to lives of despair.

As they told their stories their voices rose and ebbed in a crescendo of confessionary fervor. They developed a rhythmic syncopation to their delivery. Their interruptions had stopped but each young man was obviously eager to get his chance to speak. I asked our friend in the Oakland A's hat about his name, Little General.

He said, "My man we had guns, drugs, sex and death all before we turned sixteen. The first time I killed somebody one of my officers said I carried my rifle like a 'Little General' and the name stuck. But for true we were **ALL** Little Generals."

Throughout the civil conflicts that plagued Liberia the children, some as young as eight, were seen as an expendable commodity. The now deposed president Charles Taylor had used thousands of children during his invasion of Liberia in 1989 and again in its defense as rebels closed in around him in 2003. Sadly the use of child soldiers wasn't relegated only to Taylor's army. Rebel factions that roamed the hills and grasslands of Liberia were inundated with child soldiers.

Liberia had become a killing field and children were doing the killing.

Some of those child soldiers now stood directly in front of me filthy and forlorn. Ahead of them lay hopeless lives of begging to survive with incomplete bodies. It made me wonder if their survival had been a blessing or curse.

I had come to Liberia to work with children who were orphaned or displaced because of war. I thought I was prepared for what I would meet here. Yet, when everywhere I turned I met people eager to share their horrific stories, I realized nothing could have prepared me for this.

As the Old Testament account of a young shepherd boy named David—who slew the giant Goliath thereby saving the Israelites— illustrates, children participating in armed conflict is anything but new.

The difference is that David voluntarily offered his services in defense of his people while modern day accounts of child soldiers are more appalling. The participation of children in modern armed conflicts seldom, if ever, has the romantic trappings of a young, brave hero valiantly willing to give his life in exchange for the greater good. Children conscripted into hostilities today are stolen from their mothers' arms, kidnapped from their towns or villages, beaten, brainwashed, raped, drugged and then given a gun and told to kill. This point was driven home for me when I came across a photo of a young boy holding an AK-47, standing over a victim he had just killed. The boy had a picture of Jesus Christ on his t-shirt with a caption that read, "Jesus Just Don't Care Who I Send to Him."

That picture had come to life for me now as standing directly in front of me on a scorching November morning in Monrovia stood Double D, Captain Crazy, Little General, Original Rude Boy, and Tough Trigger Master. Could one of these men have been that boy I had seen in the photograph?

It wasn't a stretch.

Their broken bodies bore evidence of their participation in a horrific war. Still, what I saw before me now were human beings, not killers. They were homeless, but they were also temples of the Holy Spirit. They were filthy and reeked almost as much as the open sewage canal that had stifled my breath only a few minutes before; still, what I saw were brothers in need of cleaning. They smiled and laughed but what I saw was an infinite sadness.

7

Tough Trigger Master stretched out his hands wide letting both crutches fall to the ground as the young men on either side supported him. He described how a rifle-propelled grenade blew his left leg off. He spoke of the agony of losing his leg and the majority of his left buttock to the explosion. As he stretched his arms out, I no longer saw Tough Trigger Master but Jesus looking at me through the eyes of one of his wounded children.

"I didn't wake up for almost four days," he said. "When I did I was begging people to kill me-o. I was begging one of the guys next to me to shoot me in the head because the pain was so bad."

Another in the group confessed that he killed his own brother with a handgun in their village in Grand Kru County in Southeastern Liberia. A rebel commander had castrated the man's brother and chopped off his left hand. The commander threatened it would take him all day to kill the boy's brother if he continued to resist joining the rebel forces of MODEL. Instead of watching his brother suffer, the boy took the pistol from the commander's holster and shot his brother in the back of the head. He was 14 years old at the time and defecated in his pants after he realized what he had done. When I confronted him with the obvious question of why he hadn't used the gun on the commander instead of his brother, he explained that the rebels also had two of his younger sisters at knife point and their fate would have been much worse had he not complied.

Another of the men confessed that his unit would purposely target pregnant women and make a wager on the sex of the unborn baby. After the bet was placed one of the children would come out of the bush and shoot the expectant mother through the back of the head. The other child soldier would open up the victim's womb with a knife and remove the unborn baby to determine the winner. When I asked what the wager was the young man said, "A pack of cigarettes or beer."

Still another in the group remembered a game that was played involving two blindfolded child soldiers. Prisoners who had been taken by a rebel unit were lined up in front of a freshly dug grave and each of the captives was executed by a third child who used a different weapon on each person. The object of the game was for each of the blindfolded children to identify the type of weapon used to kill the captives. The child who won the contest would be excused to go eat a hot meal and then have sex with one of the older female rebels called "Teaching Mommas" who were responsible for instructing the young children about carnal matters. The loser was charged with burying the bodies. The game was called "Guess of Death."

When I asked the man if he had ever participated in the game he looked at the ground and said, "Me the best-o. I play plenty times."

After spending almost an hour with the five men I told them I needed to excuse myself and enter the grocery store. Just two months in country and any sense of innocence that had been left in me had evaporated in the buttermilk thick air of Monrovia. I was exhausted by their testimony.

Before leaving I turned to the one who had first engaged me. I asked Double D about his name and he shrugged and said it stood for Death and Destruction. He hadn't spoken much and I asked him if he had anything he wanted to say. His nimble fingers played nervously with the tenuously attached number 3 on his jersey.

He shrugged and said, "What is there to tell? We did bad, bad things, but we were young-o. We had cocaine and heroin running through our bodies and we had guns. We snort plenty brown-brown."

I knew this to be a mixture of cocaine and gun powder. "That is a potent mixture is it not my good friend?" It was more a statement than a question.

He looked up at the sky and took a deep breath then continued, "We all killed people for true; we die too in such a way, you getting me? If we were lucky we would have had our heads blown off," he said pointing an index finger at his temple, "and not our legs. The dead are back in the soil of Liberia but they the lucky ones. No boogie-man come for them during sleep. They don't see the demons-o and they don't hobble around begging for money. The dead laugh at us."

Then he turned from interviewee to interviewer, "So, my good friend, what are YOU doing here in Liberia?"

When I told them I was volunteering at a Catholic mission not far from Monrovia the men looked at me with surprise. Tough Trigger Master laughed and said, "Hey, Pa! You mean to tell me you came from the United States to work in Liberia for true?" I told them I had actually come from Honduras to work in Liberia, but they had the general idea.

Then Tough Trigger Master laughed again and said, "My good friend, you're more messed up in the head than we are." Once again he had all of us laughing.

It was a good time to make my exit.

I gave each of the guys a hug and a Liberian hand shake, where you snap the middle fingers with the person you are greeting. I bought each of them a cold bottle of mango juice and gave each of them one U.S. dollar. As they went their separate ways Double D turned and handed me back the dollar saying, "Use it for your kids so they don't wind up like us." Then he winked and said, "But I am keeping the mango juice my good friend; it's hot as hell out here."

*****

The cover of the phenomenal book, *A Long Way Gone: Memoirs Of A Boy Soldier,* written by an ex-child soldier from Sierra Leone, Ishmael Beah, carries a picture of an adolescent boy walking down a dirt path in a red t-shirt, navy blue gym shorts, and green flip flops. The right flip flop is already beyond repair. The child's head hangs a bit to the right and down and he has a forlorn look on his face. The child's head is hanging because of the weight of what he is carrying on his shoulders. He has a rocket nestled uncomfortably behind his neck that is being held in place by his arms. Dangling from his left shoulder is a rifle strap that holds an AK-47 behind his back. Bayonet attached. From his right shoulder hangs a bag that looks like it could be made to hold a laptop like the one I am using to write this sentence. But I am convinced the contents of this child's bag were far more dangerous and deadly than a personal computer. I tried in vain to clear my mind of the weaponry that the boy was carrying. Using all my background as an art teacher I envisioned the boy just in his red t-shirt, gym shorts, and flip flops – he looked like any one of the thousands of young African-American kids I had worked with on the basketball courts of Houston. He looked like one of our children at Liberia Mission on his way to clear brush from around our church or school.

In another world, he would have been downcast because he had missed two free throws that cost his team a game. Maybe a young lady had just rejected his invitation to a date. These scenarios would have been acceptable, repairable. But no matter how hard I tried to see just the boy, I couldn't separate him from his surroundings. I saw the rocket on his shoulders and the AK-47 slung across his back and the bag loaded with munitions and I knew that his sadness was infinite, everlasting. This boy, who was maybe 15, should have been worrying about mundane things. But he was so far beyond that point it made me sad. It was clear he had surrendered his childhood and the dreams that sustain it. He had given up. Then the question kept harassing my mind: "Was he even alive?" Over and over again, like an unwanted guest who refuses to stop knocking on your door, this question echoed through me.

Didn't this young man deserve to play basketball or soccer, didn't he deserve to fall in love and go to school? I closed my eyes and pictured the boy standing at his high school graduation. I pictured him next to his new bride on his wedding day. I saw him smiling as he held up his firstborn with a father's unmistakable pride. I tried so hard to will this boy into the life he deserved it exhausted me. I said a prayer that he made it.

Bowing my head just a bit lower I then prayed for the five young men on Randall Street in Monrovia and for all the young men and women who, through no fault of their own, never had the chance to be children.

Beating the Bushes

"When two elephants fight in the jungle the grass suffers"
-Liberian Proverb

I had wanted to see the jungles of Liberia from the moment I arrived in country. So here I was huffing down a dirt path barely wide enough to accommodate my Texas-sized body. This is the bush, as Africans call it, I thought acknowledging the heat and humidity pummeling my every step. But my initial awe evaporated as quickly as the beads of sweat running down my face as I concentrated all my energy on putting one foot in front of the other.

We worked our way down a dusty red dirt trail that had been welcoming travelers' feet for hundreds of years. With apologies to the legendary left field wall at Boston's fabled Fenway Park, this was the real "Green Monster." Every conceivable shade of the color danced and spun its way around and through me. A choir of trees swayed in the winds high above providing us a breezy sonata accompaniment as we moved deeper into the bush. About two and a half miles into our hike, as a thickening canopy of trees began to obscure the sun, we stopped abruptly in our tracks when we saw a clearing with a small village that looked as if it had been untouched by time or technology. We had reached our destination.

The science of life had remained unchanged here for generations. A naked baby chased after a small coconut used as a toy. Weathered African women in brightly colored lappas hunched over large wooden bowls mashing cassava into what would become the West African delicacy called fufú. A gaggle of Guinea fowl scuttled directly in front of our feet as though we were invisible – we probably were. Clarisa smiled at me and said *"National Geographic!"* But I had a suspicion that not even *National Geographic* knew about this place. In the center of the circular village grew a small thicket of bamboo plants and palm trees where several older men congregated conversing back and forth while flashing occasional, mostly toothless, smiles. One of the men spied our group and excused himself from the lively conversation.

The diminutive figure that approached us exuded a definite air of power and strength much like a lion who is ruler of the pride.

"Old Pa Flomo," he smiled sticking out his hand to anyone willing to greet him.

He introduced himself as the town chief and welcomed us to his village, which was named Frantown. At 6'5" I towered over the man yet somehow felt insignificant in his presence.

"Hello my name is Jerome," I said offering him my hand in return.

Chiseled, sweat painted young bodies, paying glorious homage to the God who sculpted them, began emerging from the surrounding jungle. Their ivory eyes studied the group of outsiders who had entered their village. Large bales of cassava and sugar cane were securely fastened to their backs and each carried a long curved cutlass. As they passed, they greeted us in a language we had never heard. I nodded back, hoping it was an acceptable response.

Old Pa Flomo laughed and said, "They don't use English too much. They speak Kpelle, the dialect of our tribe. Don't worry-o, they said you are welcome here."

I asked Old Pa how long he had been village chief and he looked past me staring into the dense vegetation while scratching his beard apparently lost in deep thought.

Then he answered, "Seventy years at least, maybe a few more."

I smiled and replied, "I didn't ask how old you were."

He looked at me quizzically and said, "I understood your question. If you asked me how old I was I would have told you 105."

After that I had no more questions.

The main reason for our trip into the bush was to bring a homesick and lonely child, Glady Sackie, to see her mother. Glady lived at our mission where she attended school, but her family lived in Frantown. For weeks she had been asking us almost daily to bring her to visit her mother and this was our first opportunity to make that happen. Glady never did reunite with her mother that day; she had traveled to a neighboring village even further into the forest before our arrival. Still the visit home lifted the young girl's spirits especially when she saw many familiar faces.

Our goodwill mission soon turned into a hands-on anthropological lesson in culture and history for me and Clarisa as Old Pa took us on a tour of his village. The women making fufú laughed when they saw how tall I was.

"Whiteman big-o, need more cassava!" said the leader of the group.

They all started chatting in Kpelle and laughing. When I asked Chief Flomo what they were saying he laughed that they wanted to be my wives. I shot a mischievous grin in Clarisa's direction.

I found the fufú was delicious as the women offered me bit after bit of the white mealy treat. Following custom, I eagerly dipped the chewy dumpling into the big pot of pepper soup that sat simmering over an open fire next to the women.

I wiped my lips and said, "Hey Ma, that sweet-o."

This elicited another round of hearty laughs, "The white man like fufú and he speak Liberian English-o!"

Next we visited the group of young men who had greeted us earlier. They were separating bales of cassava and sugar cane into two separate piles. One of the young men asked me in rapid fire Liberian English if I knew Barack Obama. When I explained I knew him well through television, books, and magazines he looked perplexed.

"But you know him-o right? You getting me-o?"

Realizing the young man was asking me if I was a literal friend of the then presidential candidate, I explained that the United States was a very big country and it was impossible to know everyone.

I asked him why he wanted to know and, washing his face and hands, he casually replied, "He plenty rich-o and he needs to buy zinc for our houses; too much money for one man."

Intrigued by our conversation, I asked Chief Flomo how the village received news and information. He said people brought newspapers to the village and, whoever could, took turns reading to their fellow villagers. There was also a lone transistor radio that was used to get periodic updates from the BBC or Voice of America, though Old Pa sheepishly confessed, the radio was mostly used to listen to soccer games and church broadcasts.

Our tour wound down at the site of a new well that had been dug for Frantown by an international aid organization. Old Pa Flomo was obviously proud of the well, but he also confided he thought it made his people lazy since they no longer had to walk to the creek to fetch the water. I nodded in agreement, as it was expected of me, and admired the structure because I could see how beneficial it was going to be for the village.

Before our group left Frantown, a young girl arrived at our party with a wooden plate of kola nut. I had heard that the kola nut was used as a traditional part of greeting visitors. I had been told that Liberians ate them to stay awake, lose weight, think more clearly and build up their energy. Assuming that the caffeine content in each nut had to be off the charts, I was interested in trying one; that is until I actually bit into mine.

My mouth exploded with a bitterness I have never encountered. Every ounce of moisture was absorbed and my tongue was left hanging like an old piece of leather.

"God this is awful," I said trying to spit out the remnants of my first bite, which had been a big one.

My face was contorted and puckered to the point my eyes shut tight. I remember hearing a roar as several old men slapped hands, greatly amused.

The ladies who had offered me the fufú were beside themselves, "Oh da' whiteman like fufú but he can't eat da' kola nut-o!"

They were right, the "whiteman" couldn't eat the kola nut but I knew I had better learn since this was a tradition of welcoming a stranger into a home or a village. The Liberians eat kola nut like we eat potato chips and peanuts in the United States.

The bitterness of the kola nut lingered in my mouth as I followed Pa Flomo back toward the dirt path that would take us to our vehicle. As we walked I asked about the effects the civil wars had on his village. Old Pa said God and the spirits of his ancestors had saved them from the brutal conflicts that devastated most of Liberia. He proudly stated that through both civil wars not once had a rebel or government soldier set foot into their world. The closest the carnage ever came to them was when they heard the distant echoes of artillery shells reducing the capital city of Monrovia to rubble 50 miles away.

Sadly very few villages were as blessed as Frantown.

*****

Nepiville is like most Liberian villages, quiet and unassuming. In fact it is identical to Frantown with the exception of its location. It lies no more than a mile off the Kakata Highway, which was the major artery for rebel movement from eastern Liberia during the second civil war. This proved to be catastrophic for its citizens one morning in May 2003.

While visiting the village one day to buy charcoal for our mission cooks, I struck up a conversation with an "Old Ma" in the village. She looked as though she was one who could speak from authority and experience. Above her left brow was a vicious scar that never healed properly leaving a long lumpy line on her face that instantly grabbed my attention. She introduced herself as Althea and it didn't take me long to realize two things. She had nothing but contempt for political systems, their agendas and the people who ran them, and she had every reason to feel that way.

"It was hard to believe in God at that time. I had lost one son in the first civil war and now I had lost a daughter and granddaughter to the second civil war. I tell you it was like the more I prayed the more I suffered. I remember one morning when a group of rebels came into our village not long after my daughter had been killed, a young woman walked out of her hut with a Charles Taylor shirt on. This woman didn't know nothing about Taylor. We were poor village people, see. It was just a shirt, that's all. Why she had it on that morning who knows? We didn't know the rebels would show up. It didn't matter. One pow-pow (soldier) walked up to her and shot her right here," said Althea pointing to her temple. "The bullet went right on through and got me here," she said pointing to her left eyebrow. "She never made a sound. She dropped right on top of me dead as dead could be. I just sat down and cried over the dead girl's body. I couldn't believe God would let this happen to Liberia again."

This type of random terror was an everyday occurrence in all parts of the bush in Liberia. If the common people didn't suffer at the hands of despots Samuel Doe or Charles Taylor, then they were victimized by those who were supposed to be rescuing them.

As Althea told me, "It was all the same-o, just a different leader, a different year but the same as before. I tell you for true-o the rebels were bad and the government was bad. The only thing Doe and Taylor changed while in office was their pant size."

What had started out as a simple search for charcoal had turned into another harsh lesson about life in Liberia. I was quickly learning that there was nothing simple about this country, a realization made all the more regrettable because it had been a beautiful country before it was forced to endure such ugliness and devastation.

As we drove back to the mission I gazed out the window at the long stretches of countryside: it seemed so calm. I wondered why anyone would destroy such beauty . What must it have been like to watch heavily armed rebels walking down the dirt road we had just traveled leading to Nepiville? How would I have felt knowing the certain calamity that would befall its innocent citizens? I asked my companion and driver Pa Alfred if what Althea had told me had happened all over Liberia.

He pulled his baseball cap down tight over his aging eyes, "All over. It happened here, it happened there, all over and it can happen again if you don't teach them children right from wrong at the mission, you getting me-o?"

I got him.

As we continued our ride I closed my eyes and silently asked God to guide Clarisa and me. We had no idea what His plan was for us in Africa. Could we really make a difference in a country so scarred by war? I dropped my window as the sun began to set. The air felt cool on my face. We still had a 25 minute trip back to the mission and I intended to use every one of them to rest my body and mind. I needed to be sharp for the kids, ready to take part in evening prayer at 7 o'clock and then to supervise study hall for the boys at 8. I looked over at Pa Alfred and he smiled at me.

"Oh the bush in Liberia, it something else I tell you."

He couldn't have been more right.

State of the Nation

"People say, "What is the sense of our small effort?"
They cannot see that we must lay one brick at a time,
take one step at a time."
- Dorothy Day

Ruined. The Ducor Hotel stood for years on the Roberts Overlook a looming presence above Monrovia; raised up, much like the crucified Christ, as a constant reminder of the ultimate sacrifice and complete destruction caused by the second civil war. From its high vista the gutted hotel was plainly visible to all who call the capital their home.

The Ducor had once operated as a five-star establishment, the most admired and busiest hotel along the entire Atlantic coast of West Africa. Its guest list was an impressive Who's Who of African and international dignitaries with the likes of Robert Mugabe, Edi Amin Dada , Halie Salassie, Henry Kissinger, Pat Nixon, and legendary African jazz musician Hugh Masekela having passed through its doors. But the day I visited it bore no resemblance to its former splendid self. Instead it looked more like a decomposing, eight-story cadaver. As I approached it from below, I felt drawn into a world that existed in a different time.

Nearby was a monument park with a statue of J.J Roberts, Liberia's first president. Just beyond that was a small lighthouse, which like the Ducor had seen better days. It had long ago given up on its original intent. Repurposed, it now provided shelter to a family of displaced Monrovians. Like the people it housed the lighthouse had fallen on hard times. Its former nobility was at present veiled by rows of drying clothes being buffeted by a strong breeze that was rising up the bluff from the ocean below.

An abandoned parking lot just below the statue of President Roberts served as a makeshift soccer pitch for a group of children. Vendors, no older than 10 or 12, surrounded me as I approached what used to be the covered circle drive that led to the reception area of the Ducor. They touted their wares: cold bags of water 5 LD—the equivalent of 14 cents in United States currency— biscuits sold for 10 to 20 LD, cigarettes 3 for 5 LD, and assorted fruit juice was 50 LD a bottle. The young vendors followed me even after my repetitive mantra of "No thank you."

One determined hawker refused to leave me. "Come on white man, buy some cold water, I beg you." Relenting I bought a bag of his water, and then gave it to him to drink. This elicited a response of, "Why don't you buy some biscuits too?"

A large UN soldier from Nigeria chased the child away as I arrived in the shade of the hotel's overhang.

"Hello, my name is Mohamed; I am from Lagos, Nigeria," came his booming voice as he approached. He stuck out his hand to greet me and I reciprocated.

Never having been to Nigeria I searched for any connection with the man I could find that would put us on common ground and allow me to gain access to the Ducor.

"Lagos!" I exclaimed. "One of the greatest basketball players ever is from Lagos. Hakeem Olajuwon played in my city, first with the University of Houston and then in the NBA with the Houston Rockets."

Mohamed's eyes brightened, "You know Hakeem Olajuwon? He is very famous with my people, very good man. He did the Dream Shake when he warred against his enemies in your basketball league."

I laughed as the large Nigerian did his best to imitate the move Olajuwon had perfected; his powder blue beret falling off his head in the process.

"Olajuwon was a very talented soccer goalie who was discovered at the Moslem Teachers College in Lagos before he came to Houston to learn basketball," I said.

Mohamed looked at me with suspicion as he squinted against the sun streaming through the large banyan trees. "How do you know about the Moslem Teachers College? Do not lie to me."

I chuckled and asked him in the same low voice, "How do you know about the Dream Shake? Do not lie to me."

A big grin spread across his face and he laughed, "ESPN of course!"

Mohamed introduced me to the rest of the Nigerian contingent guarding the ruins of the Ducor and we made small talk about the Nigerian National Soccer Team, nicknamed the Super Eagles, and their chances in the approaching World Cup. They were stunned that not only did I know who the Super Eagles were but that I knew about Nigerian soccer legend Jay Jay Okocha. Moments later Mohamed waved me through so I could start my self-guided tour of the building.

When I left the group I saw them pulling out jugs of water and prayer mats as the time for mid-morning prayers was drawing near for the group of Nigerian Muslims. While they washed their hands and feet in preparation, I turned away, letting the hotel that loomed before me cast its spell and draw me into an exploration of its wonders.

As I stepped inside what used to be the Grand Ballroom, I could almost hear the tinkling of silverware and fine crystal and see guests dancing to the mellow sounds of a big band. Shaking myself back to the present, I looked out one of the windows and saw a drained swimming pool, filled with debris and rubble. I noticed children sliding down its embankment on cardboard mats. In my mind ghostly whispers said, "I swam here in 1973. I lived here for 6 months in 1978. I played piano in the lobby for 15 years." And then: "I was thrown off the roof in 2003 for opposing Charles Taylor."

I found the staircase that would lead me up to the spot where that heinous act had been committed. Walking up the stairs I could see the Nigerian soldiers far below, prostrate on their mats in prayer. In a loud and unified voice they proclaimed "ALLAH AKBAR! GOD IS GREAT!"

The view from the roof was breathtaking. I could see virtually all of Monrovia. The east side of what used to be the Sky Bar offered the most incredible view of the capital city. It looked so peaceful I could hardly believe that just six years earlier the streets below had been filled with bands of marauding rebel soldiers indiscriminately killing anyone in their path.

From the west side of the roof I was able to take in the beautiful Atlantic seascape as well as the Freeport of Monrovia, its entrance teeming with tanker ships, silent silhouettes, waiting to off-load their goods and return to a more developed part of the world. Just below me, ringing the beachhead, sat the squalid shanty town of West Point, which Liberians say is the most impoverished area in the entire country. Even from a few hundred feet above the mountains of trash and debris were clearly visible. So were the children who were playing in and around them.

A security guard posted on the 8th floor walked over to show me the spot where ten dissidents had been shoved off the roof to their deaths on the concrete below by Taylor loyalists. There was no plaque to remember them. Their only memorial resided in the shaky memory of an aging security guard. I offered him a 100 LD tip and started back down the stairs to the ground floor.

I walked down pausing on every level. Each floor was like a page of an old dusty book longing to be read. I entered the debris-filled rooms hoping to catch a glimpse of the past. I looked out windows high above the sea and the city and was amazed at the beautiful vistas that would have once greeted the hotel's guests. Walls talk, and luckily for me the Ducor was in a chatty mood that day. Every floor had a different story to share with me. I, the solitary guest in the once splendid structure, took all of them in.

Standing in Room 612 I wondered how many people had slept there over the years. Where had they come from? What brought them to the Ducor in the first place? Two floors below in Room 455 I found an uncollected room service tray covered in years of dust sitting on a closet shelf and wondered what had been ordered, and why for that matter, the tray had never been collected. Room 309 guarded a pair of moldy tennis shoes but even through the decay I could see the familiar Nike swoosh, a reminder of the great pursuit of capitalism. I carefully approached the empty elevator shafts and while peering in I quickly realized I wasn't alone as a black bat passed close enough to my ear to startle me out of my reverie.

At last, arriving on the ground floor, which had suffered more damage than the floors above, I passed the ballroom, once again trying to imagine the long silenced sounds of tinkling dinnerware and crystal. With my mind's eye thus engaged in a game of time travel, I moved along the corridor when suddenly my physical eyes were assaulted by the all too harsh reality of the bright sunlight that now enveloped me. Shielding myself from the sun's glare, I walked to the middle of what had once been the lobby's center.

I admired a huge four-sided wood carving that, remarkably, had remained untouched by time and war. The deep cuts in the mahogany brought to life the story of pastoral Liberia. I found it ironic that the beautiful depictions in the carving represented a class of people who would never have been welcome at the Ducor. The images were of village life with mud huts that were a far cry from the comforts once offered by the hotel.

As I turned from the carving I was startled to find an old man standing right in front of me – so close that I gave out a loud cry of surprise.

"Hey American man, how da' body-o?" he said.

 I placed both hands on my knees and tried to compose myself. "You scared the hell out of me, Old Pa," was all I could muster.

His reply, "Sorry hear?" came from a smiling face with wretched teeth.

"Where did you come from? How did you know I was here?" I asked the stranger.

Disregarding my question he went right to his point, "I want to show you sumptin' white man but it's gonna cost ya' 70 LD."

He was holding some kind of portfolio in his hands and acted as though he was about to take a group of visitors on a tour of the hotel. I handed him two Liberty Dollar bills, a 50 and a 20 and asked him to show me what was so important. He led me out to the veranda overlooking the hotel's swimming pool.

"I want to show you what this beautiful lady looked like before some bad men got their hands on her," the old man said sadly.

What he produced from his portfolio were a series of professionally taken photographs of the Ducor Hotel in her heyday. There were pictures of the Grand Ballroom full of dancers and diners just as I had imagined. The man showed photos of the presidential suite and guest rooms. Friendly, smiling faces of employees and guests mingled on the beautifully manicured grounds that once surrounded the hotel. There were panorama day and nighttime shots of Monrovia and a photograph of the sunset over the Atlantic taken from the 8th floor observation decks. Finally arriving at the last photograph, I noticed it was of the swimming pool. There it was – shimmering aqua waters full of swimmers while the edges of the pool were ringed with sun bathers reclining on beach chairs and sitting under large umbrellas enjoying a respite from a torrid West African afternoon. I was struck by the stark contrast of the old photograph and the deplorable state of the pool at present.

Then I saw what the man had wanted me to see all along, that the photograph of the pool was taken from the same veranda where we were now standing.

He smiled at me as he lit a cigarette, "I took this picture in 1976 standing on the exact spot you're standing on now."

I looked at him in disbelief, "You took this picture?"

He smiled again, but this time I could see sadness, too. "I took all of them." He paused to take a long drag on his Kool Menthol and in a voice that reflected both surrender and sorrow mumbled, "But now all I do is take passport photos on Broad Street. Life changes-o."

He explained that he had been the Ducor's chief photographer for almost 20 years before losing his job because of the wars. The pain on his face was real and it burdened me, but what could I say to diminish his sadness?

"Yes," said the man. "I know this old lady better than anyone. I still squat on the 5th floor during the rainy season."

I asked about a wife and kids, wishing I hadn't, even before I finished the question.

"The Ducor ain't the only thing I lost during the wars."

The man motioned me over to the large four-paneled mahogany sculpture and pointed to a spot in front of one of the panels.

"Can you believe I took a picture of Henry Kissinger here in 1977? He was standing right where you are now. I took so many pictures of so many people but now it's just passport photos," he repeated himself with a forlorn acceptance that made an indelible impression on my heart. I wished things had turned out differently for him, for all Liberians.

"Life sure does change-o. Yes sir, it does," his voice trailed off.

I turned to ask him his name but he was gone and I was left standing alone in the spot where Henry Kissinger had once stood.

In June of 2010 the Ducor Hotel was taken over by an investment group from Libya. A three-year renovation project will cost almost

$40 million U.S. to bring the building back to her former beauty. The Nigerian UN detachment that once guarded the Ducor is gone. The only people there now are workers and surveyors who have begun the laborious task of dumping wheelbarrow after wheelbarrow of debris over the side of the building.

As I looked at the circular drive where the UN soldiers once convened I was reminded of my last visit with the Nigerians while they still guarded the hotel. They told me that when the wind was just right at night you could hear the sounds of lovers, laughter, and life from inside the old building. Then Mohamed put his arm on my shoulder and whispered, "Yes but when the wind isn't just right you only hear the screams of those who died here. It's enough to keep us on the outside."

The renovations at the Ducor are but a small microcosm of a spirited yet painfully slow renaissance that has started taking root in Liberia. When Clarisa and I arrived in September of 2008 we were astonished by what greeted our eyes. The lack of development and the destruction that dotted the landscape was abysmal. Thankfully when we departed Liberia after two years we were encouraged to see signs of life in the rebuilding effort; though small it was at least a step in the right direction.

In many ways the Ducor serves as a symbol of Liberia itself. Like the hotel, Liberia once stood as a grand and admired model of West African democracy and development. It was a destination, a place people came to visit and enjoy. But like the Ducor it was laid waste. For decades, Liberia's past grandeur has been only occasionally glimpsed through layers of decay; today these layers are being peeled away bit by bit to reveal what lies within – waiting for a chance at renewal.

Mission Possible

"Where there is no vision, the people perish"
- Proverbs 29:18

The small room used as a chapel at Liberia Mission's St. Martin De Porres Home for Boys is sweltering. Every evening at 7:00, just as the burnt orange African sunset signals day's surrender to night, boys of all sizes and ages begin gathering until all eighty-six are seated and ready to begin their worship service. The air in the room is still; hung with humidity so thick and suffocating that the children's faces and bodies are covered with rivers of sweat.

Unmindful of any discomfort, the boys begin to sway and clap to the cadence of a bush drum delivering a rhythm older than recorded time itself, marrying ancient tribal music with Christian hymns. A feeling of euphoria envelopes the youngsters as they sing with complete abandon of their Savior's love for them. Smiles fill the prayer room. A long day is coming to an end and there is much to celebrate at the mission.

Benjamin Wollor, the big brother and spiritual director for the boys living at the mission keeps the cadence of the music by clapping his hands as he meditates, eyes closed, on the scripture reading and message he will share when the music ceases. But for now enthusiastic waves of praise build heavenward glorifying God: "He is able, He is able, I know that He is able, I know that my God is able to carry me through, everywhere I go, oh Lord!"

Tonight Benjamin's message to the children is simple, turn to the Lord not just in good times but in hard times as well. Let the adversity that has plagued their young lives draw them closer to God, not drive them away. His plea resonates with all who are present that night as from the back of the sauna-like room comes a heartfelt cry, "Amen!"

The boys' exhortations are echoed just across the courtyard in the St. Bhakita Home for Girls, where the more subdued harmony of twenty-eight girls rises into the night. Untethered from the boys' energetic drumbeat, their voices glide gracefully atop the warm sub-Saharan breeze as it moves across the mission grounds insinuating itself into quiet corners like a whisper.

House Mother Mama Helena Gonyor assigns one girl to lead a scripture reading and short homily every night. This evening Serliae Johnson reads from 1st Peter; when she has finished she exhorts her mission sisters to be strong in Christ so they may stand against the snares of the devil. When Serliae compares the devil to a hungry lion looking for people he can devour the younger girls jerk to attention, eyes wide. The imagery of the ravenous lion and its devastating power for destruction is not lost on them. Serliae came to the mission a true orphan. She had seen the carnage the devil could cause up close and personal. She watched as the lion devoured those she loved.

Her village had fallen victim to a marauding group of rebels during the second civil war and she was the only member of her family to survive the tragedy. Her words were strong for a 15 year old girl but she had seen the very worst of life and was not about to let her younger mission sisters experience the same.

When the hour-long prayer session ends, the boys and girls of Liberia Mission disperse then reconvene moments later in their respective dining halls for a 90-minute study and homework session. After the last books are closed, the children retire to their dorm rooms to sleep.

The grounds, encircled by a security fence, are quiet at night, save for the occasional bark from Skippy, the resident canine. The children sleep under the watchful eyes of three nighttime security guards who keep away unwanted visitors.

The nights pass peacefully for the children, but of course, it hasn't always been like this for them: just a few years before, the promise of seeing the next morning's sunrise was often a doubtful proposition.

Even though the majority of the mission's children were young when the second civil war ended in 2003, every one of them, even those who did not suffer harm directly, has an understanding of what transpired in their country. They see the steady flow of those maimed by the war as they walk the city streets and village roads where buildings have been left to crumble and where aimless young men and women sit in the shade of broken walls. They hear the stories of death that must be told, and that can still call old men and women to weep over lost wives, husbands, and children.

Some of the residents, like Benjamin Wollor, experienced the cruelties of war firsthand. At 22 Benjamin is the oldest student living at the mission; his dream in life is to become a Catholic priest. The desire to serve God and Liberia is strong within him. But Benjamin's dream came ever so close to ending before it could flower when he was nearly killed in a rebel army raid on his village.

"MODEL came into our village in Grand Kru County and just started firing everywhere without thinking. My older brother and I were still teenagers and we knew if they caught us we would be forced to become fighters so we ran. We cleared the village; my brother and I were just a few feet apart. I saw dirt flying up where the bullets were hitting near us and I could hear them flying by my head. When I finally made it through the clearing and into the bush I turned and saw my brother wasn't with me anymore. I saw his body lying on the ground a few feet behind me and knew they had killed him. I was filled with so much sorrow. But I had to keep running."

Benjamin had other near-fatal encounters with the various armies that roamed the countryside with impunity until he eventually escaped to the Ivory Coast where his father was living and working during the war. Relocation, however, was also fraught with danger for the young man. While the majority of Ivorians were gracious and willing to assist the refugees from Liberia there were others who wanted to exploit them. Many times Benjamin was harassed by people in the village where his father lived. Food was scarce. In order to receive even a small meal of soup, rice, and bread, he had to make a day-long march to a large refugee camp that was set up to aid Liberians.

Even so, the young man's faith in God never wavered. "I didn't blame God for what was happening. He warns us in His word that there will be trials and tears in this life. What was happening was the cause of just a few men who didn't have God or Jesus in their hearts."

Benjamin was exiled from Liberia and his mother for six years.

Prior to my final departure from Liberia I celebrated Benjamin's high school graduation with him. It was a moment of intense joy for me to watch this young man finally overcome the setbacks he suffered because of the civil war. His achievement was no small matter but a feat that demonstrated to me the young man's dedication and personal courage. He is now a student at Mother Patern Polytechnic University, a Catholic college, in Monrovia. Benjamin told me that he still holds tight to his dream of studying for the priesthood.

"The one thing you learn being Liberian is patience and faith. I know God has called me to be a priest so I know that He will not abandon me," he said.

James Himmenah first came to Liberia Mission in June of 2007. James, who hails from Bomi County, also had a terrifying encounter with rebel troops. Bomi County was the headquarters of the LURD forces during the second civil war; it was also one of Charles Taylor's strategic locations for the shipping of arms and food aid to the RUF rebels whose forces Taylor was supporting in Sierra Leone.

One day when James was 10 he was taken by force from his family by rebels and carried miles away from his village. Like so many other boys of that age James was to be trained to become a child soldier. "But, I was too skinny to even hold the gun up on my own. Whenever a man would push the rifle into my arms I would fall over when he let go of it."

For two weeks James underwent indoctrination and training by the rebels, all the while making only marginal progress in the eyes of his captors. One day as James sat with a group of boys, an LURD commander, who was also from Bomi County, recognized the youngster and introduced himself as a friend of his father. The commander brought welcome news that the young boy's family was safe and had relocated deeper into the Bomi bush after their village was razed. He also said that the family believed that James was dead. It was only through the intervention of the commander that James was eventually released and returned to his family. That the boy was exceedingly lucky that this man had the will and the power to release him was evidenced by the hundreds of tiny bodies that were discarded in the bush like so much refuse. These children, like James, had been too small to be of use to their captors so they were summarily executed, their bodies dumped.

I once asked James what would have happened to him had he been forced to stay with the rebels. The young man shyly shrugged his shoulders, unwilling or unable to give an answer. "It is over now," was all he said.

*****

Serliae, Benjamin, James and hundreds of other young people who survived the brutality of the second civil war now have a chance to build a new life because of the love of others, especially one man, Dave Dionisi. While the developed world mostly sat on their hands and watched the continuing devastation that was going on inside Liberia during the final self-destructive days of the Taylor regime, Dionisi began making plans to help children orphaned by the war as soon as he could gain entry into the country. It was, he said, something he felt called to do.

When I asked Dave about his calling he described it this way: "There is a tremendous clarity that comes from living as much of a Christ-like life as you can. One of the dangers of sin is that it clouds your ability to see what God has in store for you and what you should be doing. When you are able, though, to do one good thing it gives you the strength to see the next good thing which should be done."

Dionisi had been a military officer serving in South Korea then a successful insurance executive with a beautiful wife. He had all the trappings of the American Dream. He was also a prayerful man and eventually his prayers led him to a decision: He would stop just considering his own future and begin working to transform the futures of others, specifically the poor and marginalized.

Dionisi's search for a program that aligned with his personal goals eventually led him to Mission Honduras International (MHI), a Catholic lay organization based in Chicago, Illinois. MHI was the American support team for APUFRAM (Association of Franciscan Boys and Girls Towns), a Honduran Catholic mission founded by U.S. born Fr. Emil Cook.

Dionisi journeyed to Honduras to experience firsthand the impact the mission was having on the lives of the youth in that country. Dave's visit to the mission allowed him to see that hundreds, if not thousands, of lives were being changed for the better by the work of APUFRAM. This had a profound effect on him and he returned to Honduras time and again to follow up on the progress of the children he befriended. He became one of the mission's most steadfast supporters.

The first time I met Dave was in June of 2005 when I was living in Honduras and in charge of the volunteers who regularly visited APUFRAM'S main mission site. I went to the airport in Tegucigalpa to pick up Dave and his group from the University of California at Davis for a week-long stay. Normally groups come out of the airport tired, a bit subdued by their new surroundings, unsure of what to expect or how to react. Most are more than happy to have me usher them to the mission and direct their volunteer activities during their visit. This was not the situation with Dave who shot through the terminal hand extended toward me as if we were lifelong friends, "Hi Jerome, Dave Dionisi, thank you for all the great work you are doing here for Fr. Cook," he said.

I held out my hand in return, wondering at his immediate show of warmth and confidence. I would soon learn that Dionisi was not our typical mission volunteer.

By the time we had collected all the gear and luggage his group had brought Dave had dropped into my hands *his* itinerary and the hour and a half trip back to the mission consisted of a one-on-one breakdown, day-by-day, hour-by-hour, minute-by-minute of their schedule.

I told him I couldn't believe how detailed his plans were to which he replied, "You didn't know I was an Army officer and military intelligence expert?" I wasn't surprised.

During that week I observed many things about Dave Dionisi: He had a work ethic that rivaled a computer without an "off" button. I don't think I saw him eat but a few times the entire time and I'm not sure he slept since the light was on in his room all hours of the night. I nicknamed him "The Machine."

He impressed me not only as a caring man but one you definitely would want on your side if there was trouble. At the time, I had no way of knowing that four years later Dave and I would step into the thick together.

When Dave and I talked during that week I learned that his personal mission interests extended well beyond Honduras and into one of the most dangerous countries in the world at that time: Liberia, Africa.

*****

In 2002, with Liberia still embroiled in its second brutal civil war and hundreds of thousands of people killed or injured as a result, Dave Dionisi decided he needed to do something to help. The place was, by all accounts, the worst country in the world to live, which made its case all the more urgent in his mind. He sought the advice of Fr. Cook because during Dave's many visits to Honduras the two men had developed a mutual respect and friendship. Dave shared his desire to serve Liberia and, to his surprise, the priest confided that the African republic had been the focus of his thoughts as well. Though both men had the same vision, their opinions differed greatly on the timing of the venture. Fr. Cook was hesitant to send his people into a country where safety was still an issue and would not commit to a project —undaunted, Dave forged ahead alone.

The summer of 2003 President Taylor's regime was in its death throes. Except for Monrovia, he had lost control of the country to rebel forces, which were advancing on the capital en masse. Citizens were caught between the warring armies, many of them rag-tag rebels who shot hand-held mortars into the capital indiscriminately killing any man, woman or child in their way. When UN peacekeepers finally intervened, thousands of decomposing bodies were found lining the roads into Monrovia. Charles Taylor resigned his presidency in August and fled the country. By this time three million Liberians were homeless; thirty thousand were living in tarp-covered shacks or storage containers in a makeshift tent city in the capital's national stadium. Even though Taylor was finally gone, fighting continued in the countryside where heavily armed factions tried to maintain power and would hold out for more than a year.

While others might have questioned Dave's sanity in flying into a nation still torn by war, it was clear in his mind this was the right choice.

"I believe in miracles and in angels among us." Dave once told me. "I also believe God speaks to us. I heard a very clear voice that told me to go ahead and start this program; don't wait; now is the time. That internal voice is what gave me the strength to start arranging things while the war was still going on."

Call it a stroke of luck or divine intervention, but in October 2003, when Dionisi boarded the jet that would carry him to Liberia, among his fellow passengers were top ranking officials of the incoming Liberian government who had been living in exile in the United States. Dionisi wasted no time in introducing himself to the group and explaining his intention to create an orphanage for displaced children. Before he even stepped off the plane, much of the red tape a new organization would normally have to deal with had been side-stepped, and many of the contacts he needed to establish within the government had already been made.

Dave Dionisi's bold plans for the children of Liberia started taking shape 40,000 feet above the Atlantic.

So impressed was the Liberian contingent with Dionisi and his plans for the children of their country that when their jet landed in Monrovia the American was invited to enter the country with the governmental delegation. His new acquaintances even offered him transportation from the airport to the capital in their motorcade.

It seemed to Dionisi that God indeed was opening doors quicker than he could enter them. But the surge of momentum he initially enjoyed was quickly doused by an unlikely source, members of his own Catholic faith. Dionisi recalls, "When I first came into the country I was told by one of the senior-most nuns to get back on the airplane and go home. It just surprised me that although Liberia did not have a single

Catholic orphanage at the time I was told they had enough orphanages and my idea would never get off the ground, especially with the war still going on."

While some were trying to get Dionisi out of the country before he even had a chance to unpack his suitcase, there was one very important Catholic who gave his wholehearted blessing to Dave's plans. It mattered little after that who objected because the blessing came directly from the Archbishop of the Catholic Church of Liberia, Michael Francis, a revered figure throughout Liberia for his stand on human rights and respect for the rule of law.

Dionisi fondly remembers the meeting he had with Archbishop Francis. "He was one of the few people who said sincerely, 'Thank God you are here.' He gave the program his blessing and said of the orphanage, 'We so desperately need this here.'"

Bolstered by the Archbishop's blessing, Dave pushed ahead and officially opened the doors to Liberia Mission Incorporated on November 17, 2003 in a rented space on Duport Road in the Paynesville section of Monrovia.

The mission started with a grand total of six orphans. Serving this small but challenging assembly of young children was an all-Liberian work staff of six hired by Dionisi to love and care for them. Samuel Ford Tabolo Sr., educated in England and a highly respected man in Monrovia was the mission's first Executive Director and House Father. Pa Tabolo, as he is called, showed a firm yet nurturing approach with the children. Howard Mendobar assisted Pa Tabolo with the day-to-day running of the new mission. Mary Francis Matthew was the mission's first House Mother, Augustine Nufea was head of security and the mission's technical specialist, Moses Quiah worked in the security department, and Alfred

Vah was the mission's driver. Dionisi, who lived in the United States, demonstrated a profound trust in his Liberian staff believing they could sustain and grow the mission even in his absence.

From the start, the need for the mission was demonstrated by its explosive growth. By the end of December 2003 there were 17 orphans living at the mission and within weeks the number increased to 32. By the time Clarisa and I arrived at Liberia Mission in 2008 it had relocated to a 25-acre plot in Blacktom Town, where it has its own church and school and has grown into a vibrant educational hub with over 100 resident children (no longer solely orphans) plus 250 more children attending its St. Anthony of Padua School.

Handful Kollie was one of the original six children who entered the mission that first day in November of 2003 with some trepidation. "We had no idea what the mission was going to be like. We had just seen war in Liberia. But when we realized that we were going to eat three times a day, and have a place to sleep and go to school, our fear left us." Handful is a young man of few words, choosing rather to focus on his studies and soccer but he lights up when speaking about Liberia Mission and its impact. "It makes me happy because the mission has helped so many people and it has given us the hope we need to live better lives."

Handful's thoughts and sentiments are echoed by his mission-sister Judy Massah. Judy entered the program in 2004 as a shy 10 year old and remembers the mission's original Duport Road site as being cramped and loud. "At night you heard the cars and motorcycles passing by and the people would make too much noise. The best part for me was going to school every day because it was quiet-o."

In those early days before the mission had its own school the children attended Sister Kathleen McGuire Catholic Institution, a 20 minute van ride from the mission grounds. The school was named in honor of an American nun who, along with four other Catholic sisters from the Adorers of the Precious Blood Order, was murdered in Liberia in 1992 at Charles Taylor's behest.

While Dionisi's vision was beginning to take shape in Liberia, six thousand miles away in Honduras Fr. Cook and APUFRAM were still not convinced to jump in on the venture and Dave began to give up hope that they would provide assistance any time soon.

Dave told me, "I didn't want to wait. I knew that the longer we waited the harder it would be to get the idea off the ground. But Fr. Cook and the Hondurans were very hesitant about going in-country while the war was still going on. Although I had hoped they would be interested if they saw an existing mission in place I must admit I thought the Honduran option was off the radar."

Meanwhile, the children who had been taken in by the mission began to see what a golden opportunity had been given to them and they responded. For once in their short yet complicated lives they had something they had never had before: stability.

One child who was determined to make the best of his opportunity was little Pee-Wee Sumo, one of the first children through the gate of the original orphanage on Duport Road in November 2003. Pee-Wee had lost both of his parents in the war; coupled with a birth defect that causes him to limp the boy had experienced more pain and heartache by the time he was five than most people do in a lifetime. Although the youngster appreciated the first mission site on Duport Road, he dreamed of something more. "It was too small," he recalled. And though he was grateful for the chance to go to church and school he dreamed of having a place to live where he could have space to play and roam.

While living on Duport Road, the orphans began attending Sunday Mass at St. Kizito's Catholic Church in an area known as Red Light, a reference to a long since gone stop light that once regulated traffic on the busy highway bisecting the town on the outskirts of Monrovia. Soon they were drawing the attention of the locals.

Monsignor Robert Tikpor had retired as St. Kizito's pastor but he still said Mass there and he recalls his early encounters with the orphans. "This small group of children continued to show up at Mass, the same ones every week. I thought to myself, who are these children, what manner of business has brought them to the altar of my church?"

Though he was in his late seventies at the time, Monsignor Tikpor eschewed the traditional life of retirement. He still had the fervor and energy to continue his priestly duties and the children of Liberia Mission offered a ready and willing flock in need of a shepherd.

"I saw these children and I am telling you my heart stirred within me. How could it be these children didn't deserve the very best chance at life knowing what they had already been through? I told God that I wasn't quite ready to just fade off, you know. And thankfully His response was the same."

With the support of Archbishop Francis, Monsignor Tikpor took up his spiritual duties at Liberia Mission, first in Paynesville and then in Blacktom Town. While I was in Liberia, I was amazed at the stamina of the old priest, who at the venerable age of 83, chose to climb in his car every Sunday morning to make the hour-long, bone-jarring ride from St. Kizito's to Liberia Mission over rutted, sometimes flooded roads in order to celebrate the Mass with the children, staff, and villagers who make up the parishioners of Liberia Mission's St. Michael the Archangel Church.

Today the church is the centerpiece of the mission's Blacktom Town campus and under the guidance of Monsignor Tikpor, Mama Helena Gonyor, and Mama Olivia Galama it offers instruction in the Catholic faith, baptism, communion and confirmation preparation as well as serves as home to a spirited church choir composed of mission children and directed by Mama Helena.

In the improbably short span of under three years, Liberia Mission transitioned from a tiny rented structure in Paynesville, Monrovia to the 25-acre campus it now occupies in Blacktom Town in Lower Careysburg. For this to have happened at all, let alone so quickly, was due to hard work, synchronicity of goals, and determination.

Dionisi, always the driving force behind Liberia Mission Incorporated, was pleased when in November of 2005, Fr. Cook and APUFRAM, finally convinced of the safety of the country and the viability of the mission, sent two Honduran members of APUFRAM to assist with the running of the mission. At long last the Honduran "experiment" that Dave had hoped for was unfolding. The duo to arrive from Honduras, Hector Lanza and Norman Nunez, brought a wealth of knowledge in the areas of agriculture, manual labor, and construction. This would serve the mission well given that the topography and weather of Liberia is much like that of Honduras: hot, humid, and tropical. The two men arrived prepared to help the mission with much more than growing a greener garden. They came fully anticipating that they would direct the mission as well. The hope was that they would institute some of the same strategies that had contributed to the success of APUFRAM's programs in Honduras.

I was still living in Honduras at the time Hector and Norman were preparing for their two-year commitment in Liberia. I remember Fr. Cook asking me if I could help the two with their English since that is the official language of Liberia. I was happy to help any way I could. Luckily, both of the men had an acceptable grasp of English so I thought it would be a breeze to help them prepare. Little did I know until I set foot in Liberia myself three years later that an acceptable grasp of English meant absolutely nothing. Even for me, a native speaker, the English of Liberia is a patois that demands careful listening and is still difficult to comprehend at times.

Like me, Norman and Hector were going into an unknown world hoping to do God's work. They were leaving behind families—in Hector's case a wife and three young daughters. But I had faith that if I, a displaced American living in Honduras, could make it as a missionary in a strange land then they, too, would succeed in far-off Liberia.

With Fr. Cook and APUFRAM now committed, Dionisi was able to convince the board of MHI in the United States to help support Liberia Mission with funds and volunteers. This, in turn, raised the international profile of the mission.

MHI jumped onboard wholeheartedly, even though their workload was now doubled. The board, directed by four people in particular, John Dewan, Bob O'Dwyer, Tom Teeling, and Joanie Fabiano, began working in earnest to correlate their efforts between the U.S., Honduras, and Liberia. Finally, it seemed that the survival of the little mission was assured – an assumption that would be sorely tested.

By 2006 the Duport Road location had served its purpose. The site had grown obsolete and insufficient for an international operation. With funding now coming from Mission Honduras International, its

U.S. supporters, workers arriving from Honduras, and the mission's growing reputation inside Liberia, Dionisi felt it was time to broaden the organization's vision.

"We just outgrew the site at Duport Road. It was clear that the mission was something the Liberians wanted and needed so we decided to dream big, which is something you really need to do in a situation like ours," he explained.

Dionisi had been preparing for the expansion for some time, arranging the purchase of the 25-acre plot of land in Blacktom Town using his own finances the year before. The site Dionisi chose for the new mission was more than an hour's drive from the capital and promised a quiet, pastoral environment for the children. No longer would they be disturbed by the nightly noises of a crowded, boisterous city. There was just one problem: The site was overgrown with vegetation, thick jungle vines enveloped the property making it impassable. The new home for Liberia Mission would take a lot of work.

"I remember the very first time I saw the land, I thought Lord Jesus we are going to have to build jungle houses way up in the trees and swing around on vines like Tarzan," laughed Helena Gonyor. "I thought what have they done, we are never going to be able to build here."

The clearing of brush began with help from Harris Mulbah, Augustine Nufea, the children of the mission, and villagers who were hired as day laborers. On Fridays and Saturdays the workers would step into the thick vines and begin swinging their machetes, clearing the dense jungle foot by hard-won foot. No matter how daunting the task they were determined to see it through to completion.

Even venerable Pa Tabolo, at the age of 71, got into the action showing up occasionally with his machete. "Can you believe at my age I was walking through the jungle in knee boots clearing the land?" he chuckled. "But I wanted to because with every swing of the machete I could see one more block being laid for the children of the mission."

Harris Mulbah remembers how simple the operation was, "The van would drop us off on the side of the road and we would just hop out, walk into the bush and start working. The thing I remember most about clearing the brush though was the heat. It was too much."

"Everywhere you looked people were swinging machetes," said Augustine Nufea. "Many people worked to finish the job. There were many, many machetes and it was long, too long-o, but look what we have now."

Once the ground was clear a small army of men with shovels began to dig, preparing a foundation of sand and gravel that would be followed with hundreds of pounds of concrete. All construction work in Liberia is painstakingly done by hand—no backhoes, no tractors—unless you are fortunate enough to be funded by the United Nations or a foreign government—we were not. Work proceeded for many months, concrete blocks were piled one atop another, slowly rising from the ground until one day the first structure was complete. It was, fittingly, a school. St. Anthony of Padua School opened its doors on September 11, 2006.

It seemed that excitement about the construction at the mission spread to other quarters as well when a respected priest, Monsignor Andrew Karnley of the Archdiocese of Monrovia came to the mission one day and weighed-in on the prospective church's design suggesting that the existing plans be upgraded to include office space, a conference room, and a covered porch. It was counsel well-given. Mere months after the school's completion St. Michael the Archangel Catholic Church, additions included, welcomed Monsignor Robert Tikpor and the surrounding communities for its first Mass.

Next, construction began on separate complexes for boys and girls. These were to include space for the House Mothers and Fathers, Honduran workers, and volunteers to live as well as administrative offices and a kitchen. The mission complex was expansive to say the least, a far cry from the confines of Duport Road and Paynesville. With only a portion of the acreage developed, there remained room for even further expansion when needed.

On May 12, 2007 Liberia Mission Incorporated locked the metal gates at Duport Road for the final time and made the move that had so eagerly been anticipated. When the children arrived at their new home they were elated; none more so than the little boy who had been praying for more room to play, Pee Wee Sumo.

*****

The mission continues to grow, upgrades seem to be constant. There now is a chain-link security fence topped off by barbed-wire encompassing the entire front half of the compound. A sign on the Kakata Highway identifies the mission to passing motorists. A concrete laundry area provides a place for the children to wash their clothes, not by machine but by hand—one bucket for pre-rinse, one for wash, and the last for rinsing. The children have grown expert at twisting and wringing excess moisture from their laundry then hanging it to dry on one of the many rows and rows of clothesline strung like non-functioning Christmas lights throughout the complex.

A sixty foot water tower sits directly behind the boys' home and contains two five-hundred-gallon water drums that supply the mission with clean water for bathing and cooking and just behind the water tower sits fifteen acres of fertile farmland that is actively cultivated and tended by the mission's children and workers. The farm produces almost twenty different varieties of fruits and vegetables that are consumed by the children and sold at the Red Light Market by the mission's staff.

Liberia Mission has come very far in just six years. Because of the recent surge in interest from people in the United States and Central America wishing to visit the mission, ambitious plans are being made to build a thirty-two person visitors' dormitory. In addition construction has begun on a new mission site outside the city of Buchanan, the capital of Grand Bassa County, a five-hour trip by car from the Blacktom Town site.

In 2009 the mission welcomed its first volunteer group when a dedicated medical team of fifteen arrived from Florida, South Carolina, and Montana to direct medical clinics in and around the greater Monrovia area. In just one week the group provided two thousand Liberian men, woman and children with much needed medical care.

The mission has finally become the international organization that Dave Dionisi hoped for. Even as its reputation continues to grow abroad it has remained a local force, providing work, education, and spiritual direction for countless numbers of Liberians.

February 24, 2010, was a hallmark date for all those in attendance; I was proud to be one. Coadjutor Archbishop Lewis Zeigler and Monsignor Andrew Karnley visited St. Michael the Archangel Church to celebrate a special mass of dedication. In his closing remarks Monsignor Karnley addressed the congregation, which was at capacity, and proclaimed, "Liberia Mission Incorporated is absolutely the best thing that has happened to Liberia since the second civil war ended in 2003. Its presence can't be overstated, its impact can't be measured enough and its future can't be bright enough."

Her Name is Musu

"Whoever causes one of these little ones who believe in me to sin, it would be better for him if a great millstone were hung around his neck and he were thrown into the sea."
-Mark 9:42

The relentless February sun beat down on my bare head, but I didn't mind. I'd been in tropical climates for five years now and I found the day beautiful. Smiling, I sang an old Jimmy Buffett song, "The Last Mango in Paris." I sing when I'm content—songs by Buffett and Hendrix and the greats of another era. I had been heading for my room where Clarisa's tasty lunch of fish and rice awaited me. Our air conditioner was running though it was mid-day. I saw this unexpected bonus as a chance to take a short nap in relative comfort. Normally electricity is strictly rationed to the early morning and evening hours so I was not about to let this mid-day treat go uncelebrated.

Halfway there I remembered that I did not lock the door to the clinic so I turned and started back around the shaded courtyard. A few steps from the clinic door I saw a girl dressed in our school's Kelly green jumper, and, unmindful of the heat, bundled into a grey sweater. Her white knee socks were bunched around her ankles and she played nervously with the sweater's zipper. Her head hung low, buried for the most part in the sweater so that I could not immediately identify who this child was.

I thought I recognized her, though I did not know the girl well. "Musu?" I asked tentatively.

The girl cleared her throat then in a voice so fragile I almost didn't hear her she said, "Can I speak with you, Uncle Jerome?"

A warning sounded in my head.

"Director Omar has been doing bad and wicked things to me," she said.

With the warning now blaring I suggested, "Let's go into the volunteers' kitchen where we can talk." I couldn't bear the thought of another child stumbling into this conversation.

Once safely inside I wanted to make sure I had heard correctly so I asked, "Director Omar has done bad things to you, Musu?" She nodded. "Do you want my help?" I said.

She looked at me. Tears ran unabated down her cheeks landing softly on the dry fabric of her sweater where they were quickly absorbed, swallowed like a momentary cloudburst in a dry desert. Her eyes, swollen and full of fear and shame held mine for only a moment then she looked away.

"Can you do something to make it stop?" she pleaded. "I want it to stop."

I searched for the right words. But a sense of growing alarm and anger made it difficult to think. Finally I said, "Musu, whatever Omar has been doing to you is not your fault. You are a child." Then I added that Clarisa and I would do everything we could to help her.

I hoped my feeble words would at least temporarily relieve her of some of the shame she was carrying like a physical presence. Perhaps my words helped. She seemed less agitated as she informed me that she had asked her parents to come to the mission the following day. Musu then asked if Clarisa and I would join their meeting. I assured her we would and that I would sit by her side the whole time if that is what she wanted.

"Thank you, Uncle Jerome," she whispered then turned towards the girls' dormitory. As I watched her retreat, her thin back hunched under a weight she could hardly bear, my heart broke.

Walking back to my room I no longer had Buffett or Hendrix or any song in my head. The sun, earlier my friend, now beat down upon me relentlessly. When I finally made it to our door I almost could not summon the energy to turn the handle. I felt drained, burdened by Musu's words.

When Clarisa saw my face she knew something distressing had happened. I held onto her tightly as I recounted Musu's allegation. Ever the pragmatist, Clarisa cautioned that we needed to wait until the next day to get a clearer picture of what had happened. Musu's accusation surprised her as much as it did me for we had believed up until that moment that Omar was doing an excellent job as administrator of Liberia Mission. Further, I had recently sent an email to Mission Honduras International in Chicago attesting to the fine work Omar had been doing in Liberia.

Omar Orellana and Alexis Rodriguez had arrived at Liberia Mission in 2007, the successors to Hector Lanza and Norman Nunez who, having fulfilled their two-year commitment returned home to Honduras. Alexis proved to be a disastrous administrator and was recalled home early, but Omar? He was great—at least that's what I thought.

That night sleep would not come. In a heightened state of anxiety I tossed in bed as Musu's words played in an endless loop in my brain, "Director Omar has been doing bad and wicked things to me."

What sort of things? I wondered. But my mind would not let me go there just yet. All I knew for sure was that I was going to make things right. Whatever it took.

The next afternoon Clarisa and I arrived at the girls' dormitory at 2:30 and were mildly surprised to see the number of people already gathered. Musu's mother and father, seated on folding chairs, looked unsure of why they had been summoned by their daughter. In a show of family unity, an older brother and sister were there, too. Housemothers Helena Gonyor and Olivia Galama along with housefather Harris Mulbah sat solemnly while, apart from the others, Musu rested on the concrete steps, her back leaning on a pillar for support. There was an air of expectation as I sensed the group was not quite complete.

A moment later, Omar walked through the gates of the girls' compound looking anything but composed. He shook like a malaria patient. It was obvious that he knew what was coming.

Even so, he cast a sidelong look at Clarisa and me and challenged: "Y ustedes por que estan aqui?" Why are you here?

Clarisa shot him the look of a lioness about to pounce as she replied in an equally challenging tone that Musu had asked us to come. "Por que ella quiere que estemos." Because she (Musu) wanted us here.

It was clear we were headed for a confrontation.

Mama Helena leaned towards Musu who was facing away from Omar unable to look at him. "Musu, tell us why we are here," she said gently to the girl.

The child, only 14, summoned every bit of her courage and began speaking but her voice failed her. She began again. She fixed her eyes firmly to the ground as she told of how Omar had, on three separate occasions, forced himself upon her, raping her violently. She told of fearing that she was pregnant and being told by Omar to take abortion pills he had provided her. She told of being threatened with expulsion from the school and the mission if she told anyone about what was happening.

I looked at Clarisa in astonishment. I wanted to stop my ears. Bile rose in my stomach. I looked at Musu's mother—her head had dropped onto her chest. Her father stared blankly ahead, eyes fixed on nothing. I looked at Musu, though she trembled as she spoke, compared to Omar she was an oak.

When Musu finished we sat in silence. Then Clarisa, once again the lioness, asked Omar if what Musu charged him with was true. "She is speaking the truth," he admitted, but he added that this was his problem and that the girl wanted sex. "Si, dice la verdad, pero este es mi problema y queria el sexo tambien."

Switching to English, Omar tried to defend himself by saying that Musu had wanted the relationship and was, therefore, partially to blame. It was a hollow, self-serving defense that convinced no one.

In fact it only added fuel to an already explosive situation.

I waded into the fray. Figuring that this was no time for niceties, I asked Musu point blank if Omar had completed the act of intercourse with her. She said he had. I asked if she wanted to be with Omar in this way.

"No, I never wanted this," came her answer. "But he threatened to put me out of the mission if I did not give in to him."

I asked if she was a virgin prior to this. She said she was.

That was when the meeting exploded. First Clarisa then Musu's brother jumped to their feet shouting at Omar.

Musu's mother, who had a better command of her native Kpelle tongue than she did of English, sat quietly, tears streaming down her face. Perhaps she did not know all of the words spoken that afternoon but a mother can recognize the pain in her child and she understood well enough what had just been said.

Musu's parents had survived the atrocities of war and the depravations of poverty; I would never know how much they suffered. But here, now, was the ultimate betrayal. Because at our Catholic mission they had assumed their youngest child would be safe, would be cared for. And they had been wrong.

We sat together – alone in our sorrow. A great evil had entered the mission and we trembled at its touch.

Mustering control of himself, Omar, defiant showman, rose to leave as if still master of his destiny. "I have work to do," he said and strode through the gate without a backward glance.

When the meeting ended, Clarisa and I went back to our room, unsure of what we should be doing. No such doubt crippled Musu's family, however. They hurried off to the Mount Barclay police station to press charges against Omar.

Omar, meanwhile, went directly to the mission's office. He had a very limited window of escape, maybe an hour before the police would show up, but he did not flee. Instead he cocooned himself in his office in the company of two of his fellow countrymen, Hondurans he had been training to take over administration of the mission when his commitment ended the following month. Emin Rodriguez and Roger Montez were the third pair of administrators sent to Liberia Mission by APUFRAM.

Clarisa and I, finally finding our balance, hurried to intercept Omar. We came upon him in the tiny headquarters flanked by Emin and Roger. The already crowded room shrank to even smaller proportions as we entered. Upon his desk we could plainly see two newly written checks totaling $7,000 U.S. drawn on the mission's account at Eco Bank Ltd. I could perceive but one reason for these checks—they were meant as bribes to assure Omar's freedom from arrest and prosecution.

The idea that bribes would be given to officials in Liberia came as no surprise to me. In my experience, bribes constituted an everyday way of doing business in this still-broken country. What galled me was that Omar was stealing from the mission, robbing the funds generously donated by our supporters for the care of our children. He was taking bread off the table of the mission's kids. I wondered just how those in the United States would feel knowing their money was going not to feed and educate children but to bribe a rapist out of jail.

Clarisa attempted to short-circuit the imminent theft by telling Emin and Roger that Omar had confessed to having sexual relations with one of the students, which at the very least constituted statutory rape. If she thought to gain support from the duo, she failed. Their expressions said it all: they had no intention of abandoning their friend and countryman.

Omar, like a rooster strutting in the courtyard moments before his neck is wrung, seemed oblivious to the seriousness of his situation. Perhaps at that moment he was unable to grasp that what he did was not only morally reprehensible, but also illegal. Arrogance buoyed him up and overruled his better judgment. He told Clarisa to be quiet. He told her that none of this was her concern and that Emin and Roger were now in charge—in effect they were her bosses and she was answerable to them.

I had remained silent throughout this exchange but with this display of machismo toward Clarisa and the earlier revelations, Omar lost all claim to respectability and I saw with crystal clarity the very real harm he was doing not only to Musu but to all of the children at the mission. On top of that, his callous actions were placing every non-Liberian worker at the mission in peril. It wasn't just his neck now on the chopping block; it was all of ours.

A verbal tsunami washed over me. Every derogatory name I had ever learned in Spanish sprang from my lips. I had no desire to control or limit this outburst. It felt good. It was the release I needed for being duped. For five months Clarisa and I had lived next door to a child rapist and called him our friend. I felt a fool for not having suspected anything. I felt betrayed. But most of all at that moment I felt rage.

I am not a small man. Always, before, I tried to mitigate my size and put others at ease by cultivating a mild manner. But not here, and not now. Doubtless at that moment I was frightening to behold.

Before I could do real damage, a better angel grabbed hold of me and escorted me out the door and into the sunlight. I walked the perimeter of the courtyard trying to quell my anger. Slowly I put one foot ahead of the other, crying as I walked, taking no notice of where I was going until I found myself once again in front of the director's office. This time my better angel fled before my fury. I strode through the door pulled back my right fist and with all of my might landed a roundhouse punch on the side of a filing cabinet.

The satisfying sound of crunching metal greeted my ears. My hand stung badly but at that moment I hardly felt a thing. Omar looked at the dent in the cabinet with a shocked expression—shocked I suppose that it was the cabinet and not him that was the target of my wrath.

Believing my anger to be spent, he cocked his head in my direction and said, "Si me va a matar hagalo ahora." If you are going to kill me, do it now.

I laughed at him and told him that death would be too easy a punishment – then I spit in his face.

And just like that I became small, like him.

******

In the end, Omar waited too long to make his escape. A contingent of police showed up at the mission just as school was letting out. In front of more than 300 students, teachers, and others the director of Liberia Mission Incorporated was handcuffed and led away in disgrace to the Mount Barclay police station.

My fury long since spent, I felt satisfaction at the thought of Omar incarcerated, every vestige of arrogance knocked out of him.

In short order, I learned that, as before, he admitted to having sex with Musu but justified it by claiming that she was 18 and not the 13-year-old girl we knew her to be at the time of the rapes. Like us, the police were unconvinced by Omar's assertion. A doctor's exam revealed that the child had vaginal bruising and scarring so two charges of aggravated rape were added to the original count of statutory rape. With these new charges Omar faced the very real possibility of life in prison if convicted.

In the days and weeks after the arrest, suspicion, fear, and finally panic worked their way through the mission. Events unfolded quickly as further transgressions were revealed. With Omar safely behind bars, staff and children came forward to tell their stories. They told of how prostitutes had been brought onto the mission grounds, and girls in surrounding villages brought allegations of rape against Omar. I heard of the director's excessive drinking and of his driving children, especially girls, off the mission grounds unsupervised, returning hours later.

The only reprieve from the deplorable situation that was unfolding was Musu was not pregnant. While this was welcomed news the damage had been done, Omar had robbed a beautiful girl of her virtue.

Why, I wondered, had no one noticed this happening?

I got my answer when several employees confessed that they had known of many of these infractions—even the rape of Musu—but did nothing to stop it.

I wanted to rush to judgment and condemn their inaction. That is, until I heard the whole story. Everything, as they say, in context. Here is our context. Liberia is a war-wounded country still stepping back from the brink of destruction. For years, survival was the only thing that mattered to most people. This mindset still exists and though people no longer fear for their lives, they fear losing their livelihoods. In a country with no social safety net this is a very big concern because without a job a person faces the very real possibility of going hungry. In these situations accommodations are often made; silence easily bought.

But, of course, that is not the whole story. There were brave souls who did try to speak up, four of them; and it is the knowledge of what happened to them that effectively sealed the mouths of the others.

During the summer of 2008, just prior to Clarisa and me coming to Liberia, Fr. Emil Cook, who was the spiritual director of Liberia Mission, was paying a two-week visit from his home in Honduras. Since accepting Dave Dionisi's invitation to become involved with Liberia Mission Incorporated in 2005, Fr. Cook had managed two annual visits; this was his third. The priest was proud of his affiliation with the Liberian mission, prouder still that members of his organization APUFRAM were now sending administrators to Liberia, an outreach the priest called, "third world countries helping one another."

Father's visits were greatly anticipated by the children, volunteers, and employees of the mission – this year more so than ever. Towards the end of his stay, four Liberian staff members approached the priest with their concerns. They confided to him that they worried about Omar's intentions towards some of the girls; one in particular was named Musu.

Father assured the four that he would take matters in hand. Unfortunately, Father's touch was very light. The day after the priest was safely out of the country, Omar, still in charge and unbowed, confronted the four employees who had spoken to the priest and fired each one of them. I learned of this only after Omar's arrest.

*****

With Omar in jail, I felt that I had to inform Fr. Cook of the events unfolding in Liberia and ask for direction on how to proceed. But Fr. Cook was in the United States on his annual fundraising tour and try as I might I could not reach him. I left many messages to no avail. To make matters worse, word of what Omar had done was beginning to spread throughout the surrounding community and things were growing ugly.

As I stood outside the Barclay police station the day after Omar's arrest, a crowd of 70 locals gathered calling for his release so that they could deal with him according to the "law of Moses." I began to hear rumblings, threats to take over control of the mission site. Now I was worried – very worried.

Since I couldn't reach Fr. Cook I tried Manuel Cartegena, executive director of APUFRAM in Honduras. No answer. All around me the crowd continued their hostile murmurings.

Finally, I made the one call I wanted to avoid. I called Mission Honduras International (MHI) in Chicago. I was taught by Fr. Cook that whenever problems arose we were not supposed to involve the people in the U.S. His stock phrase whenever there was trouble was, "Oh, I hope the people in the States don't get wind of this." Only this time we weren't dealing with mere wind but with a category 5 hurricane that was quickly bearing down on us.

When I heard the familiar voice of Joanie Fabiano, stateside director of MHI at the time, I felt like a lifeline had just been tossed to me from halfway around the world. I grabbed onto it with both hands.

Little did I know at the time that my lifeline was about to ensnare Fr. Cook and APUFRAM.

As I stood outside of the police station, I told Joanie of the rape accusation and Omar's part in it. When she had processed the news, she promised to bring this matter to the immediate attention of MHI's board and get back to me with further guidance. I hung up with Joanie and felt somewhat better for having finally informed someone of our delicate situation at the mission. I didn't want to be standing in the midst of this mob any longer. There were too many voices raised in anger and contempt though I could also hear voices of reason emanating from some in the crowd. I hoped these would be the ones to carry the day.

Discretion being the better part of valor, I quietly headed for the truck and returned to the mission. If we were going to head off further trouble then I had people to talk to, namely the town elders and Governor

Tom Dennis of Blacktom Town. Once I arrived back at the mission and parked the truck I crossed over the highway and headed toward Governor Tom's home. I felt the sting of a thousand eyes on me as I made my way through the village.

My plea to the elders was simple: We volunteers didn't deserve to suffer because of Omar's gross lack of humanity. Besides myself and Clarisa, I felt I was speaking for Emin, Roger, and Matt Hayes, a volunteer who had arrived from the United States just one week earlier. I tried to impress upon Governor Tom and the elders that we loved the children and were in Liberia for the right reasons, to serve God and the people. Governor Tom reassured me that no harm would come to any of the volunteers including Omar. With the immediate crisis of our safety averted, I felt a huge weight lift from my shoulders. I was grateful for the restraint showed by the village leaders, though I cared less about Omar's well-being at that moment than I did about the safety of the rest of us.

With no imminent threat to our welfare, it was now time to think about how we could go about repairing the damage Omar had done not just to Musu but to the entire mission community.

Though Clarisa never voiced the shame and embarrassment she felt because a fellow Honduran had been the source of such a horrid act against a child, I knew that she was suffering because of it. I also knew that this would propel her to even greater action in an effort to lessen the harm caused by Omar and I loved her all the more for that.

As it turned out, her countrymen Emin and Roger would also be propelled to action but in a different direction, placing them at odds with the rest of us as they stood squarely on the side of Omar and APUFRAM. Their decision didn't surprise me though. I had suspected from the moment Omar admitted to his repugnant crime that those who ran APUFRAM in Honduras, Fr. Cook included, would most likely circle their wagons in an effort to redirect blame and control the damage to their organization regardless of the sinfulness of this course of action. Sadly, I was right about this.

Within four days of Omar's arrest Dave Dionisi, now a board member of Mission Honduras International, was dispatched to Liberia to uncover the truth of the allegations against Omar. Dave was uniquely suited to the task not only because he had founded the mission six years earlier and maintained close ties with the children and personnel, but also because he had an understanding of the country's culture and a background in army intelligence. He would not be easily fooled.

Very shortly after his arrival Dave went to the prison where Omar was being held to interview him. Once again Omar admitted his transgressions, but he also tried to defend his actions with the same old argument that Musu was older than everyone believed and wanted a relationship with him. He begged Dave for help. Help, Omar would learn, would not be coming any time soon because at that moment people were crying for justice.

Dave stayed at the mission several more days interviewing staff and children. To his dismay he learned that one of the original orphans to be taken in when the mission was established in 2003, Esther, now 11, had been expelled by Omar. Esther, it seems was strong-willed and Omar feared that if she learned of his attacks on Musu she would not be cowed into silence. Dave, knowing the character of the girl set out to find where she had gone. It took some time but upon discovering Esther living with an "auntie" in a rather remote village he reinstated her immediately.

I informed Dave that the problems at the mission did not end with Omar but also included his banished countryman and former administrator Alexis Rodriguez. This I am proud to say I had a hand in.

Clarisa and I had been in country for only about two months working as volunteer teachers at the mission school. The oldest student living at the mission was Benjamin Wollor. Benjamin, 20 at the time, was still in high school not because he was unintelligent; on the contrary he was bright, motivated, and hard working. He was still in high school because his education had been interrupted by years of almost constant civil war and the complete collapse of the country's entire educational system. Benjamin had suffered great personal loss, too. He had seen his brother killed and on two occasions he was forced to kneel on the ground with a gun pressed to his head, moments from execution. Only when a rebel commander recognized him as the step-son of a former ally was he allowed to live. He fled to the Ivory Coast, living the life of a refugee until it was safe to return home.

Benjamin was also extremely devout and a dedicated "big brother" to all of the younger boys living at the mission. Through all this Benjamin had kept the hope alive that one day he might be allowed to study for the priesthood. This is the young man that Alexis chose as the focus of his prejudice.

I personally witnessed on more than one occasion how Alexis went out of his way to provoke a confrontation with Benjamin, then, the clash begun, Alexis would use his position of authority to humiliate the young man and hurl obscenities at him. It was as if Benjamin embodied everything that Alexis disliked about Liberia and its residents. He never wasted an opportunity to call, not just Benjamin, but the all the children dogs, or worse. These displays were despicable. A final showdown came when Alexis, in a fit of pique, demanded that Omar expel Benjamin.

It was either that or Alexis would return home to Honduras.

I was not about to watch this young man's bright future erased, which it surely would have been, by an unbalanced person in a position of authority he never should have had. I called Fr. Cook in Honduras to alert him of the problem. The priest was personally acquainted with Benjamin having counseled him on his decision to enter the seminary. He was surprised by Alexis' unearned ire towards the youth. To his credit, Fr. Cook must have set the wheels in motion for the recall of Alexis for not long after the Honduran returned to his country, and Benjamin remained at the mission.

This was the Fr. Cook that I knew and loved. Unfortunately, this was not the man I would come to know in the months that followed.

Upon his arrival back in Honduras, Alexis was awarded the coveted position of director of the APUFRAM mission site in San Jose. Though I found that troubling at the time, I was happy to have him out of Liberia.

When Dionisi completed his inquiries at the mission, he returned to the U.S. and submitted a written report on his findings to members of the Mission Honduras International Board. To say this caused a stir would be putting it too mildly. The board called itself into emergency session and met for ten straight hours discussing the report and how to deal with the problems in Liberia. The situation in Liberia was grave but the situation in Honduras appeared to be even more acute as board members reexamined past reports that had come to them about abuses in Honduras. These prior claims of abuse and irregularities, some several years old, had not been given much credence mostly because Fr.

Emil Cook steadfastly defended his operation and his people. The man had built up such an impeccable reputation with those who believed in him that his word was taken as gospel.

I, for one, could fully understand this serious breach in oversight.

Father Emil Cook, born in Kansas in 1939, has been a Franciscan missionary since the early 1970s. He started numerous schools, orphanages, student housing projects, and helped erect churches across much of Honduras. He is omnipresent, traveling the mountains and rugged country roads from central Honduras to the Caribbean coast three days a week saying Mass and visiting children at the various APUFRAM sites. As he travels from one small town to the next people often line the roads waiting for his white van to give them a lift to the local church. Everywhere you turn there are individuals and families who have benefitted from the priest's interventions over the years. Those who love him are legion. His loyal followers and supporters in the United States are nearly as devoted to him as those he has helped raise out of poverty. That is the man I got to know during my four-year stay in Honduras. That is the man I looked upon as not just Father, but my father.

One of my fondest memories of my time in Honduras is of waiting for Fr. Cook to arrive at the Volunteer Center in El Conejo, where I lived with several other long-term volunteers, so that we could join in the celebration of the Mass. The center is located about a 10-minute drive from the town of Flores where Fr. Cook has his main compound. I remember standing at the kitchen window with a cup of strong Honduran coffee in my hand and watching for the priest's truck to make the corner of the Pan American and La Paz Highways. Like a child I waited at the door so that I could be the first to greet him. Being in his presence was to be in the presence of a living saint—or so I thought.

The fall from grace is a messy prospect. The higher the pedestal you have been placed on the more damage one encounters when they topple. Fr. Emil Cook had a very long fall.

My actions the day of Omar's arrest still haunted me. I was ashamed for my outburst so I resolved to make amends. I would visit Omar in prison. Though I hated the things he had done, I still saw him as a child of God and vowed to follow Christ's teaching in the Sermon on the Mount when he said, "If you are offering your gift at the altar and there remember that your brother or sister has something against you, leave your gift there in front of the altar. First go and be reconciled to them."

I prepared for my visit to Monrovia's Central Prison by packing some food, water, and juice into a bag. It was a ritual I would perform a total of five times, the number of visits I made to Omar while he was in prison. During my 90-minute stays, Omar often described his life behind bars. It was appalling.

The prison itself was in deplorable condition, designed for 300 inmates it housed closer to 800. And though it sat but 100 yards from the beachfront, the heat and humidity in the institution was unbearable. There was no ventilation to speak of and outside light never made its way into the cells. Meal times were held in such a frenetic atmosphere as to make a barnyard look orderly by comparison. The feeding ritual entailed the employment of a 30-gallon trash bag to hold a gelatinous mixture of gari, a grits-like food staple eaten by the people in West Africa. Sometimes fish heads or tails or even an occasional piece of grizzled meat would be added to the jumble. When ready, the trash bag would be tossed unceremoniously into the center of a room holding 40 or more prisoners. No utensils, no tables, no marks of civility at all. The hungry would attack the bag with dirty hands in a wild free-for-all.

This was the sorry state in which Omar Orellana lived for almost four months until his unceremonious release on June 7, 2009. He never did come to trial for the charges made against him by Musu. Some contend that this was for a lack of evidence. I don't believe that—there was plenty of evidence to assure Omar would spend many years behind bars. What happened is that a generous amount of what is called "cold water" money changed hands between people in Honduras and Liberia enabling Omar to scurry home the moment he was released. It's not unusual. As I said before corruption is endemic in this West African nation.

Did he suffer enough for his crimes? Only God can decide that question.

But one thing I do know for sure is that there were those who should have known better who applied relentless pressure on Musu to change her story during Omar's months in prison. I, too, was vilified for my role in this drama. I don't know just how far the plot went and I can't attest to all of the people involved but I do know that a group of Catholic nuns from Brazil, Colombia, and Spain living in Liberia conspired with Omar's friend Emin Rodriguez as well as others to get Omar released from prison. I believe that this plan also reached back to some U.S. supporters of Fr. Cook and APUFRAM, and most sadly I believe Fr. Cook was behind this pressure.

I learned from Musu that a rather unholy cabal of nuns had visited her in an effort to get her to say that she had lied about Omar and about her age. They wanted her to say that she was 19, not the 13-year-old child she had been when she was raped. They wanted her to say that she desired a sexual relationship with Omar.

When I heard about this visit, I went to see Musu to encourage her to stay the course and not be influenced by outside forces. Even though Musu had by now come to forgive Omar, she could not retract her accusation.

To do so would place unearned shame on her, her family, and her village. In the end she would not retract her charge. I was proud to stand by her. I knew how she must have felt facing down a group of women she had been taught to respect as spiritual guides and teachers in our Catholic tradition. I knew because the nuns had also paid me a visit.

These same women had come to me to plead for Omar's freedom. They wanted me to convince Musu to change her story and when I would not they labeled me Judas. I could not understand at this point all of the machinations that were taking place to gain the former director's release. All I knew was that there were those within my own Church who would see injustice done to a child in an effort to gain a guilty man's freedom. Those who had been entrusted to protect Musu were the very ones hurting her. The nuns' appeals to change my testimony called into question their motives. I viewed them as willing to defend the interests of Fr. Cook and his beloved APUFRAM by trampling on the truth. Were these really representatives of my Holy Mother Church? My faith was in tatters – what little there was left of it fled out the door on the heels of the departing nuns.

For the next several months, pressure continued to be applied almost relentlessly on me as well as Musu. Through friends in Honduras and the United States I learned that my reputation was being muddied with accusations against me personally. Associates of Fr. Cook portrayed me as trying to undo his decades of good work by painting him and APUFRAM as guilty of knowingly covering up past crimes. And the atmosphere at Liberia Mission continued to deteriorate.

A child had been raped and when it became apparent a cover-up was to follow I blew the biggest, loudest whistle I could find. I had made a promise to Musu to protect her. It was a promise I was intent on keeping regardless of personal costs.

There was one Catholic priest who, in my mind, rose to the occasion: Monsignor Andrew Karnley, the helpful advisor during the construction of St. Michael's Church. The monsignor had taken an interest in Liberia Mission, believing it to be a wonderful influence in his country. Though he was deeply troubled by the accusations of child abuse at the mission, like Clarisa and me, he felt the best course of action was a full airing of the charges. He was a pillar of strength for us and in the months following Musu's revelation we became good friends, valuing his counsel and support.

The monsignor visited the mission often during this period, sharing meals with Clarisa and me. When we were in Monrovia we would take him to lunch at Flocee's Restaurant, our favorite place to sample authentic Liberian fare.

One day, over a meal of potato greens and fish the monsignor leaned over towards us and said with conviction: "It does not matter how much mud the Church gets on itself because of this. We are doing things the right way! The Church has and will continue to survive." These words were water to a thirsty soul. The Catholic Church of Liberia was going to stand on the side of a defenseless victim. Many times Monsignor Karnley had ministered to me and Clarisa but none more than today. With my faith in the Church and humankind bolstered I said a prayer of thanks for this man of God.

Still it didn't mean I wasn't struggling with my doubts.

Ultimately my belief in Christ prevailed. In large measure Clarisa rescued my faltering faith when one night she said, "Just think if we had not come to Liberia, Jerome. Musu would still be being raped. God put us here to stop this."

At that moment I felt with every fiber of my being what it meant to be an instrument of God.

The downward spiral in relations between Mission Honduras International and APUFRAM only accelerated after Omar's release from prison and return to Honduras. A forty-year ministry began to unravel as Fr. Cook's Conventual Franciscan Provincial back in the U.S. was called in to mediate between the two groups that had worked together so successfully for decades. The hope in the U.S. was that with the Franciscans involved an adequate child protection policy could be put into place not just in Liberia but in Honduras as well where as many as two dozen accusations of abuse had surfaced.

For months the groups danced back and forth, trying to make something work between them. But the rift grew too large to mend. In April of 2009 APUFRAM recalled Emin and Roger to Honduras, washing their hands of Liberia completely. The next month MHI informed Fr. Cook and APUFRAM that without a proper child protection plan in place it could no longer help raise funds for their operations in Honduras; though MHI would accept sole responsibility for the mission in Liberia. It was at this point that the board of MHI asked Clarisa and me to step in as co-directors of Liberia Mission to guide it through this turbulent period. We did this willingly, though not without apprehension. We knew full well that our best efforts would be needed if we were to restore the integrity of the mission in the eyes of the children, staff, and surrounding community.

When Emin and Roger abandoned the mission after just four short months in Liberia they left a place awash in uncertainty. The night of their departure Clarisa and I joined the children in evening prayer and it became clear to us that Musu was not the only child in pain. The boys and girls, many with tear-stained faces, sat quietly as we tried to reassure them that the mission would stay open and that they would continue to have a place to live and be educated. I hoped my words were true.

When the prayer session drew to a close I started to walk towards the door of the chapel, then I heard a voice say, "Uncle Jerome, are you and Auntie Clarisa going to leave us, too?" The question pierced my heart.

I have no idea who spoke the words but it felt like Christ was asking me, through one of our young boys, to make a commitment. It was then I understood we wouldn't be leaving Liberia any time soon.

The Franciscans attempted to bring Fr. Cook back under their umbrella. Ultimately these efforts failed. Fr. Cook was too entrenched in Honduras and too emotionally invested in APUFRAM. After all, he had created the organization and staffed it with grown men he had known since childhood. Men he had nurtured and taught. He was not about to cut ties with them even if they were guilty of abuse or malfeasance. I think, as Fr. Cook has said more than once, he is more Honduran than American now.

Though the U.S. Conference of Catholic Bishops has forbidden Fr. Cook and APUFRAM from soliciting donations in any manner in the U.S. they manage to skirt the issue by no longer making appeals in churches. They have, in effect, become a secular organization. Fr. Cook stays on at the mission he founded, defying his Order's demand that he remove himself to Saint Joseph Cupertino Friary in Comayaguela, Honduras.

These facts fill me with sadness. Fr. Cook has fallen from the pedestal I once placed him on—his kingdom toppled by a little girl. Her name is Musu.

A Trinity of Sorrows

"O grave, where is your victory?
O death, where is your sting?"
- 1ST Corinthians 15:55

They say tragedies come in threes—the first proof of that arrived late in 2009 as the mission was still struggling to work through the chaos created by Omar's arrest and ultimate release from prison. At the time, Clarisa and I were beginning to feel that we were finally making headway in restoring people's faith in the mission. We were almost ready to breathe again. Then, in quick succession, three members of our mission family unexpectedly died, plunging us once again into an extended state of shock and sorrow.

I took little Elijah Koko's death the hardest because it should never have happened.

My friendship with the 10-year-old began on the day he taught me how to eat sugarcane and I have never had a more memorable lesson in my life. It was a lesson given fairly early in our stay in Liberia while Clarisa and I were still adjusting to the country's often withering climate. We were assigned as teachers in St. Anthony of Padua School.

I had a kindergarten class and so did she. Elijah Koko was one of my students.

Every day little Elijah would bring a large stalk of sugarcane to class. On a particularly unforgiving day of heat and humidity, during the middle of a lesson, I was overcome with dizziness and thirst. I sat down unsteadily in a folding chair hoping to regain my balance. Elijah noticed my discomfort and came marching up from his table at the rear of the room carrying a reed of sugarcane three times his height.

"Here Uncle Jerome, eat this; it has juice," he said.

He quickly broke a small part of the stalk off with his foot and handed it to me. I had never eaten sugar cane before and I didn't know what to do with it. I opened my mouth and tried to gnaw the rough fibrous grass. Part of the hard shell casing splintered from the stalk and poked me in the mouth causing a sharp pain in my right cheek. I let out a yelp that brought a cascade of laughter from my class. Elijah rolled on the floor, slapping his knee. He couldn't stop laughing and neither could the rest of the students. His amusement, finally spent, Elijah got to his feet and grabbed the sugar cane from my hand.

"Here Uncle Jerome, like this," he said.

Then the boy made quick work of the piece of sugarcane that had just moments before been a source of pain for me. Ripping and tearing at the stalk Elijah was soon enjoying the juice contained within the plant.

The abundance of juice that came from the stalk was more than enough to quench my thirst. The sweet, sugary nectar was better than I had expected and gave me a jolt of energy that enabled me to get through the rest of the school day. As the children were leaving, Elijah approached and asked where the remainder of the sugarcane had gone. I smiled sheepishly and told him I had eaten the whole thing.

"Oh, Uncle Jerome ate the sugarcane small and liked it too much and ate the whole thing!" Then he extended his little hand. "5 LD please, I need to buy more sugarcane at the filling station."

I handed him the requested amount, trying hard not to laugh at the serious expression on his face as he waited for payment.

We left the classroom together parting ways at the door. Elijah headed to his home, which sat directly across the street from our school, and I headed straight for my room to try and brush the sticky, sweet sugarcane juice from my teeth before it could do permanent damage.

Over time, Elijah and I grew close; in part because we shared the same sly sense of humor that others often didn't understand. Though Elijah did not live at the mission, he was a beloved member of our extended mission family.

When Clarisa and I took over as directors of the mission after the departure of Emin and Roger, it was with some regret, since we would be leaving behind our teaching duties at the school. It was hard for us because we had built close and loving relationships with our students.

During this time, Elijah and I still saw one another often. Whenever I went to the school to talk to the principal or a teacher we would always seem to bump into one another. When I walked across the highway or to the soccer pitch adjacent to the mission grounds we would make a special point to visit. Whenever the subject of the sugarcane came up, Elijah would break into a deep and hearty laugh that was so infectious we were soon both gasping for air.

Of all the non-resident students, Elijah was my favorite. And then, suddenly he was gone. The manner in which he died still haunts me.

Unknown to either me or Clarisa, Elijah had developed a staph infection in his throat that the locals call "risings." A rising is a puss-filled boil that usually appears on the surface of the skin and can be lanced and drained daily while administering a simple antibiotic like amoxicillin; something we had in abundance in our mission clinic. Elijah's mother, however, had little faith in "white man's" medicine; an attitude that, sadly, is not that uncommon.

On a Wednesday evening, having already missed two days of class, Elijah was eager to get back to school and his first-grade classmates. He told his mother that he wanted to go to school the next day. Opting for traditional "bush" medicine, Elijah's mother prepared herbal tea full of pepper and roots that would help burst the infection in his throat. Before retiring for the night Elijah drank the mixture, a short time later his mother reached deep into the boy's throat and popped the boil with her index finger; then she sent her son off to bed. What she did not realize was that while the boy slept, the infection began draining into his throat, poisoning him.

The next morning Elijah awoke, bathed, and dressed for school. But he could not eat breakfast, complaining to his mother that he did not feel well. He walked outside where he fell to the ground in front of their hut and began to seize. David Fannie, Elijah's uncle and a security guard at the mission, witnessed the seizure and flagged down a passing car, rushing the boy to a hospital operated by Doctors Without Borders. But by the time they arrived at the hospital the boy had lapsed into a coma. He never regained consciousness.

Later that morning, as Pa Alfred and I were about to start off on our daily foray into Monrovia, our school principal, Benjamin Glee, flagged us down. Then he told us the tragic news about Elijah.

Pa Alfred let out a long sigh that seemed to say, "Not again, Lord."

My reaction was more physical. The strength drained from my legs and I found I could no longer stand so I dropped to the ground, crouching in the dirt. Clarisa, who had been standing on the front steps of the boys' home, saw all this from a distance and quickly realized that something was terribly wrong.

With a shaky voice that was on the verge of breaking I relayed the news to her, "Mr. Glee just told us that Elijah Koko died this morning."

With that once sentence, she, too, was drawn into our circle of grief.

American filmmaker Todd Looby, a guest at the mission for the past month, was working on a documentary about the history of Liberia Mission Incorporated. Todd was planning to use his last full day in Liberia to follow Benjamin Wollor at his high school, St. Kizito's, in Red Light. But Elijah's sudden death quickly changed his priorities. Todd and I both realized that we needed to honor my young friend; what better way, we thought, than to memorialize him in the documentary? When we asked Erasmus Koko, Elijah's father, for permission to film his son's final journey, he agreed without hesitation.

Though Todd did not know Elijah well, the child's sudden death affected him deeply and his empathy for a family in tremendous pain was evident throughout that interminable day as he discretely filmed the rituals that surround bereavement in Liberia.

All through that long day I went through the motions of what was expected of me without registering the finality of what had happened to my young friend. My first duty was to see that Elijah was brought back home. By mid-morning a contingent of five of us gathered to begin the somber journey to retrieve the child's body from the hospital morgue.

Pa Alfred, Elijah's father, Elijah's uncle Christopher, Todd, and I made the torturous ride with hardly a word spoken among us, each of us grieved in silence. When we finally arrived at the hospital, Mr. Koko was enveloped in layer of grief so thick it crippled him and he could not bear to go inside. While Pa Alfred and Todd stayed by the truck with Mr. Koko, Elijah's uncle and I went to claim the body. David Fannie, the uncle who had taken the boy to the hospital in the first place, met us as we made our way to the morgue.

That day the morgue was filled with about fifteen bodies, all of them children ten and younger. I passed an infant not yet covered whose glassy stare sent shivers through my body. I had to force my eyes away but everywhere I looked there were small bundles – waiting to be claimed. The smell of antiseptic hung heavily in the air, turning my stomach. We moved deeper into that room of death, each step harder to take than the last as if the dead were pulling at us, begging us to linger a bit longer. I understood why Elijah's father stayed out in the sunlight – anyplace but here.

I thought of how sorrowful today was going to be for so many families in the area.

Finally we came to a small wrapped body and the nurse, who was assisting us with great empathy, identified it as Elijah's. I took a deep breath and said we needed to be sure before carrying it to the truck. Knowing the problems that exist in Liberia, claiming the wrong body at a hospital was very much a possibility. When David reached down and opened the sheet to expose Elijah's face, sorrow washed over each one of us; we began wailing as one.

Elijah looked as though he was just asleep, not dead. I couldn't believe he was dead. His little body was dressed for school in his St. Anthony of Padua t-shirt. He looked like he should be sitting in his first grade class—not lying here. David fell weeping into a chair. I held Elijah's Uncle Christopher; brothers in sorrow, we, too, cried uncontrollably.

Then David stood up and beat his chest, "My God, damn this nonsense; everyday has to be a mountain-o. Damn it."

As we carried Elijah's body towards the truck, Mr. Koko broke into long, rhythmic pleas, "Why God? Why? That's my boy-o. That's my boy. Is this fair? Is this fair? Is this fair-o?"

I hugged him close, enveloping his small thin frame completely in mine and said, "Pa, sorry-o, I love Elijah. He is with God now, Pa."

I knew this was a feeble attempt at comforting him but it was all I could muster. I looked over at Todd who had been filming throughout. He had the camera in front of his face but that wasn't enough to hide the tears streaming down his cheeks.

We brought Elijah's body back to Blacktom Town so the villagers could mourn his death. School had been cancelled and the village was filled with hundreds of people. When the village elders raised the child from the back of the truck, Elijah's mother broke free from the group and sprinted toward them screaming unintelligibly. Two men restrained her before she could grab the body.

For the first time, I thought I wasn't going to be able to make it through one more day in Liberia.

Elijah's classmates cried and called for their little friend to come back to them. David Fannie's daughter, Marthilyn, who was in Elijah's class, ran to me and threw herself into my arms.

"Uncle Jerome PLEEEEASE bring Elijah back. Oh, please don't let him die," she wailed through bloodshot eyes.

I felt powerless. All I could do was hug her remembering that a few months earlier the girl herself had been nearly killed by a taxi as she crossed the highway that separates her home from our school. As a result she endured several painful surgeries. Neither of us could know that fate had an even harsher blow in store for her. But this day, with no foreknowledge of what the future held, Marthilyn cried for her lost cousin and best friend, Elijah Koko.

Mourners gathered under a palm-thatched veranda to pray and share reflections about Elijah. As the mission director it was expected that I speak as well. I didn't want to talk but I had no choice. I rose slowly and looked into the faces of those gathered.

"Elijah taught me how to eat sugarcane one day ..." Then I broke into tears. I have no recollection what I said after that.

Elijah had risen at 7:00 a.m. He was pronounced dead at 8:26 a.m. and by 2:20 p.m. he was being covered by the red-clay of Liberia.

As we were leaving the grave that was still only half filled, I noticed that the burial workers had brought a small supply of sugarcane with them. I asked one for a piece of the sugary treat that Elijah loved so well. Walking up to the muddy hole that was the child's final resting place, I thanked the boy for bringing so much joy into my life. Then I chewed off a piece of the sugarcane and tossed the rest of it in with my friend.

****

Elijah's death wounded us all, none more than David Fannie, the boy's uncle who was with him when he died.

David came to work for Liberia Mission in December of 2008 as a night-time security guard. Like Elijah, he lived directly across the street from the mission in Blacktom Town. Besides being a friendly and helpful man, David was always ready for good conversation. Countless nights we sat out under the moon on the front steps of the boys' home talking about whatever came to mind. I would always have something new for David to eat from the volunteers' kitchen. He loved dried apricots, something he had never eaten before. He also had a weakness for Campbell's tomato soup with rice.

I had developed a habit of calling him Cuba because of his uncanny resemblance to actor Cuba Gooding Jr. When I called him Cuba, David always answered with a pleasant, "I beg you to show me a picture of this man."

One night I produced a picture of the actor and, noting the resemblance, David laughed, "Do you think he would change places with me, Uncle Jerome? I think he has a lot of money."

David was a good employee who cared greatly for the children, but he was also a troubled man who kept his sorrows hidden deep inside. Still, I knew some of his worries: the death of Elijah weighed greatly on him and after that sorrowful November day, David never was quite the same. Problems with his wife and finances played with his emotions as well. He lived in a small two-room hut that was home to him, his wife and their four children. Because Marthilyn had been in my kindergarten class, David and I were closer than I was with the other employees at the mission.

As much as Clarisa and I enjoyed having David as an employee most days, there were several times that we had to call him into our office and confront him for coming to work in an inebriated condition. David swore every time that this would be the last time we were going to have to address the issue, yet it would invariably prove untrue.

It all came to a head one night in April of 2010 when Clarisa came into our bedroom and said, "I think David is drunk again. We can't keep warning him about this."

Of course she was right. Though we felt we had given him every opportunity to straighten himself out, without fail every month or so he would come onto the grounds intoxicated. This night when I went to confront him I found him standing in the chapel lecturing the resident boys. Something was very wrong; David had never approached the children like this before. He was rambling incoherently and was obviously in a disheveled state, even more so than previous times. As I entered the room determined to put an end to his confusing sermon about failures in life, he abruptly stopped talking, spun around and walked right by me toward the exit of the chapel.

Then, as if just seeing me for the first time he asked, "Hello brother Jerome; how are you?"

When I responded that I was fine he shot back, "I'm fine, too, praise Jesus." Then he left.

To be sure that I was judging David's state correctly, I asked Amy Spelz and Mat Travis, two new volunteer members of our staff, if they had noticed his odd behavior. Both were in agreement that he was intoxicated. I informed them that I was going to send David home for the night so he could get some sleep and sober up.

When I arrived at David's post on the front steps of the boy's home, I noticed that he had fallen over trying to sit in his chair and was just then steadying himself. I asked him to walk with me. We made small talk as I led him toward the front gates of the mission where I finally broached the subject of his drunkenness.

"David," I said, "I want you to go home for the night, splash some water on your face, eat something, sleep, and come back to work tomorrow sober."

My words were stern, straightforward and direct, but all the time I had my hand on his shoulder.

I continued, "David you know we like you. The kids like you and you have been a big help to us, but Clarisa and I are tired of warning you about coming to work intoxicated."

Edwin Paye, the front gate security guard for the night, came over and lent me his support, "Jerome is right-o. You can't be in front of these children like you are. Go on home now and come back tomorrow like the boss man said."

I patted David on the back and told him we would talk the next day. It was the last time we ever spoke.

Harris Mulbah, the house father for the mission boys, rarely if ever knocked on our bedroom door before 7:30 in the morning. So when I opened the door at 6:15 and he was standing in front of me I knew something was wrong.

"Uncle Jerome you are not going to believe this but somebody just called me from across the street and David Fannie hung himself this morning," he said excitedly.

Another tragedy had knocked on Liberia Mission's door and it was getting to be more than we could bear.

The unenviable job of identifying and taking photos of David's body, as well as assisting the police in their investigation, fell squarely on my shoulders as well as Mat's. It was a regrettable baptism under fire for the newcomer and it quickly erased any notion he may have harbored that Liberia was in any way an ordinary country assignment. My soul was heavily burdened. I was thankful that Mat was by my side that day. There was no way I could have made it through the day if he hadn't been.

In the end, after talking to those who worked and lived with David, it was apparent he had been planning his suicide for some time. It turns out that his rambling sermon to the mission's children the night before was a goodbye. The boys told me he had begged them not to fail at life like he had and not to walk away from God. The villagers in Blacktom Town revealed he had lectured his children, especially Marthilyn, that he would not always be there with them so they needed to have a strong faith in God and needed to support each other.

The worst injustice in David's suicide was that his daughter Marthilyn was the one who found him. Just like the day Elijah died she came running into my arms screaming and crying when I arrived to identify the body.

"Ohhhhh, Uncle Jerome my Pa is dead-o, my Pa is dead."

I was angry that this little girl had suffered so much in the span of 10 months. I held her tightly, not saying a word. Then I passed her off to Harris as I entered David's home and headed toward the small bedroom. I saw David's legs first, stiff and rigid. I had to duck underneath them to see his face and, once again as in the morgue, dead eyes looked right through me.

"Forget praying for him his soul in hell-o. He killed himself."

The voice came from somebody I didn't know as we stood in a steady, cold downpour watching David's body being lowered into a hastily dug shallow grave. Suicide or not, judgment is left to God alone and I was going to pray over his body. I stood at the foot of the grave and asked Christ to have mercy on David's soul. I figured he had lived in hell already. It made sense that he deserved a break.

David's words in the morgue the day we claimed Elijah's body echoed in my memory.

"Every day has to be a mountain-o. Damn it," he had cried.

Looking into his muddy grave, I tried to understand just how hard it must been for him to attempt that climb every day. When he finally grew too weary to take even one more step, he simply gave up and allowed despair to dictate his final act.

As I turned to leave I noticed a gaunt figure holding a shaking umbrella, "Thank you, Uncle Jerome, it was a good thing you did there."

I made small talk with the man for a few minutes and then bid farewell, "I have to return to the mission, Mr. Kamara. We have plenty of work," I said.

He smiled and waved goodbye and I moved off not knowing that within weeks, he, too, would play a part in this trilogy of death.

Mohammed Kamara was a soft spoken and kind man. He wasn't Liberian by birth; he had been born and raised in Freetown, Sierra Leone. He once told me that he left Sierra Leone to escape the many problems of his country. I asked him how that had worked out; he smiled at my sarcasm, saying that though he picked the wrong country to come to, at least he had a steady job. Whatever the circumstances that led him to Liberia I was grateful because he was a good teacher and his students loved him.

In May of 2010 Bernardine Ileto and her husband Dr. Brian Chan arrived in Liberia to relieve me and Clarisa of our administrative duties. We were going home. Bernardine was the new director of operations and Brian, being an M.D., would provide health care for the children, employees, and volunteers of Liberia Mission. I remember having called Bernardine the day David Fannie died. It was a courtesy call to inform her of the tragedy but I also wanted to drive home the point of the possible problems she would face as the new mission director.

Clarisa and I had the trip of a lifetime coming up. Not only were we going to celebrate our second anniversary in South Africa we were also going to enjoy the World Cup, as the Honduran national team had qualified for the historic event. Their long and grueling journey had been rewarded with a place on soccer's biggest stage and we wanted to be there to cheer them on. The plan was to train Bernardine and Brian for a month, then hand over the administration of the mission to them completely, leaving on our trip with light hearts.

Our journey took us first to Ethiopia and then South Africa. On our flight from Monrovia to Addis Ababa I told Clarisa that I thought we had seen the end of our tough times and that our last few weeks in Africa would be smooth.

As we sat in an internet café in Johannesburg checking e-mails, I opened one from Bernardine. While an English fan slapped me on the back congratulating me on the U.S. equalizing 2-2 against Slovenia, I discovered I had more bad news to share with my wife.

"Clarisa, Mohammed Kamara died."

My lovely caring wife looked at me, her eyes held mine a brief moment, and then she sighed and just shook her head. The news of Mr. Kamara's death brought back the memory of the day we buried David Fannie. I saw him waiting with me and Clarisa like a silent honor guard until the last shovel of dirt covered the hole where David was laid.

It made me wonder if he had known that his time was short.

As is frequently the case in Liberia, the cause of Mohammed Kamara's death was a mystery. The circumstances surrounding it were frustrating, but given the man's reclusiveness not entirely unexpected.

The teachers at St. Anthony of Padua had become concerned when he had missed class and a teachers' meeting without contacting anyone. But they had no one they could call to check up on the man, for Mr. Kamara had been a solitary figure without obvious friends or family beyond the school and mission.

Concerned, Dr. Brian Chan went to Mr. Kamara's home where he found the man in an unresponsive state. Brian arranged for him to be taken to Saint Joseph's Catholic Hospital where care was to be provided. In the days that followed, Brian made several calls to the hospital and was assured that Mr. Kamara was well enough to be discharged and returned home. Still, no one at the school or mission had heard from him so Brian decided to follow up with a visit to Mr. Kamara's home, only to find it empty. There had been a clerical mix-up at the hospital, not all that uncommon. The teacher had died shortly after being admitted. All the while the people of Liberia Mission—apparently the only ones who cared enough to check —were being told that their colleague was recovering when in truth his body way lying, unclaimed, in the hospital's morgue.

When Brian and Bernadine finally learned of Mr. Kamara's death, they saw to it that his body was claimed and returned to the village where he had lived in Liberia; laid to rest in his adopted country. Unlike Elijah's, or even David's, death, Mohammed Kamara went on his final journey with only a few to mark his passing. No mass of villagers turned out like they had for Elijah, nor did he have close family members as David had to remember him and shed their tears at his death. Though his mission family remembered him, it didn't seem enough.

As our time in Africa drew to a close, Clarisa and I found ourselves increasingly looking forward to our move to the States. For me, it would be a return home, for Clarisa it would be the beginning of a marvelous new life. Liberia had been difficult. We really had not anticipated how severely our resolve would be tested. It would be good to finally reach the safety and comfort that awaited us.

Even though I was excited, guilt became my uninvited companion as we returned to the mission to pack and bid our goodbyes during our final weeks in Liberia. I knew we would be leaving behind a country steeped to its core in sorrow. It is a place with almost insurmountable problems: short life expectancy, scant education, astronomical unemployment, corruption— the litany goes on and on. We had done our best for two years, but it was not enough, not nearly enough.

Ignorance, despair, and loneliness had contributed to the deaths of three people I held dear. It was a somber finale to our Liberian experience.

Leaving Liberia

"Some people feel the rain. Others just get wet."
-Bob Marley

We had packing to do. In a couple of days Clarisa and I would be leaving for the U.S. and there was still much to do before we would be ready to give up our home of the last two years, not the least of which was preparing the children for our departure. Clarisa was being very efficient in organizing what we should take with us and what we should leave behind – I felt superfluous for the moment so I decided to take the opportunity to do a little organizing of my own by reflecting on our time in Liberia. Like Clarisa I was trying to decide what I should pack up to take home and what needed to be jettisoned; only I wasn't worrying about what socks to pack but what memories.

Without a doubt there were triumphs, perhaps the biggest was assuring the mission's survival. But there had been disappointments, too.

Elijah's death was catastrophic for me. I think about him every day – I must admit that at first it was hard to get past my anger at the senselessness of his death. If only: if only Elijah's parents had sought medical treatment for their son; if only people were better educated; if only people could be pulled out of their poverty. Mercifully, time was working to dissipate my turbulent feelings enabling me to remember my young friend for the joyful, though fleeting, gift he was. My thoughts drifted to David's suicide and Mohammed's lonely passing and I decided to add them to the "If Only" column on my Liberian balance sheet. Finally, I let my mind travel where I had forbidden it to go over the last several months – to the cruel rape and heartless treatment of Musu at the hands of my "brothers and sisters" in the church. The failure of Fr. Emil Cook to show the spiritual fortitude necessary to lead us through the crisis left me with unresolved doubts and unanswered questions. However, as with Elijah's death, time and distance were proving to be good medicine and I was beginning to let go of some of my anger.

Liberia held some sweet memories as well.

The friendships we had built and the love we had experienced from the children and staff were rooted securely in our hearts. I would especially remember my friend Pa Alfred, our driver. We spent so much time together we became a complementary set, like ebony and ivory. I even started calling Pa my African father.

To which he laughed, "I like that you see me as your Pa. It's honorable but oh my, you are too white!"

This was the kind of humor that we shared and it kept us both in stitches most of the time. After a while, Pa Alfred also became my teacher.

On a morning shortly after my first visit to the bush class was in session for me once again. My assignment was to fill the mission truck with diesel for the upcoming week. Simple enough, I thought, but as I was to learn nothing is simple in Liberia. I was just finishing a cup of strong coffee and a breakfast bar when I noticed Pa Alfred looking at me through the kitchen window. "Yes sir, correct, we gonna go fill the tank correct?"

I bid Pa Alfred good morning and asked him if he wanted a cup of coffee.

He just shook his head, "Liberians don't need coffee; gives us the shakes. We eat the kola nut instead of drinking coffee."

My mind instantly went back to my first encounter with kola nuts and Old Pa Flomo in Frantown. I had a mental shiver; I felt the same way about the kola nut as Pa Alfred felt about coffee.

Pa and I made small talk as we drove down the Kakata Highway toward Monrovia. We spoke about soccer and the Honduran national team. It surprised Pa, and most Liberians in general, that a substantial number of blacks played for Honduras. I went on to explain to Pa about the Garifuna people.

The Garifuna are descendants of Island Caribs, (a mixture of native and South American people) and a group of West African slaves. They mainly live in Honduras and Nicaragua and to a lesser degree in Guatemala and Costa Rica. The largest community of Garifuna people in Central America lives along the north coast of Honduras. Like the Kru tribe of Liberia they are seafarers and fishermen living in coastal communities. Much of their culture, including religion, music and tribal customs can be traced back to West Africa.

Pa Alfred was amazed, "My God, Honduras has black people. I never imagined such a thing." He had become my teacher on all things Liberian, so I was happy I could impart a small history lesson about Honduras to him.

Then he smiled and slapped my leg, "Black people in Honduras, my God." I could tell he was tickled by that information and it made me smile, too.

As we were finishing our conversation, Pa pulled the truck into a small roadside stand near an area called Cooper's Farm, which was about a fifteen-minute drive from the mission. I was confused because we obviously were not at a gas station. All I saw were jars of what looked like apple juice sitting in rows of ten on concrete blocks.

I asked, "Hey Pa, what are we getting here, something to drink?"

He parted his lips in a wide grin exposing his white teeth, a perfect contrast to the deep, smooth ebony ruts of his face. "Hey man, this ain't no juice," Pa said slapping my knee. "This ain't no juice for us to drink. This here is the diesel for the truck. Give me 2,000 LD."

I realized then that the rows of glass jars were full of diesel, not apple juice. Soon a young man appeared and jammed a large plastic funnel into our gas tank and began pouring the contents from one of the containers into our truck.

"Hey my man, diesel clean today boy?" Pa questioned the attendant.

"Diesel clean, Old Pa," said the young man.

Pa offered a warning to the young man. "Don't want to come back, you getting me now?"

"No worries Old Pa, diesel clean," was the half-hearted reply to come from the back of the truck as the attendant gave his attention to pouring fuel rather than conversation. We paid the young man and drove away. I asked Pa if this was the way it was all over the country.

He laughed again, "Hey man, you have too much to learn about Liberia."

At 80 I figured I couldn't ask for a better teacher than Pa Alfred.

The smallest lessons like this one were often the most moving.

These were my thoughts as I toured the mission compound, cup of coffee in hand, for a final time. Pausing in my reverie a bit too long on one of the dirt paths, I experienced a sharp pain in my right foot —fire ants! Now that was something I would not miss at all. In my head I heard Clarisa's perpetual warning about the dangers of wearing flip flops out into the foliage.

As I neared the soccer pitch I could see a game was going on among some of our younger children. They darted back and forth in hot pursuit of a half deflated soccer ball. Shadows stippled the horizon as the day was coming to an end. I stood there a few moments enjoying the bucolic scenery. There was a sudden explosion of activity as a dozen little figures, in heedless pursuit of the ball, seemed to collide at once, falling to the ground in a heap, bodies strewn in the dirt. For just an instant I had a visceral reaction to the scene – is this what a killing field had looked like? I heard a few whimpers and moved a bit closer accompanied by the mission's dog, Skippy. The dog's investigation of the melee was short-lived involving a few strategic sniffs before he turned back the way he had come to seek the comfort of the kitchen.

Children began untangling scraped arms and legs, a split lip or two was in evidence. Tears left tracks on dusty faces. Yet within a few moments all had regained their feet and began reforming their teams. Once again they moved fluidly up and down the field – a goal elicited a somersault of joy and high fives from teammates. I smiled and backed off. They didn't need my help. I took a mental snapshot. I wanted to remember this moment – it was definitely going home with me.

I turned from the soccer field and headed back to our room; it was time to help Clarisa. One final picture played in my mind as I walked – it was of five young men, each dressed in American castoffs. They were as I first met them, leaning on crutches, telling stories, laughing, their shattered bodies temporarily forgotten in the company of fellow travelers. Then the picture shifted slightly and only four were left. On my last trip in to Monrovia I learned that Double D had died a few days earlier.

"What was his real name?" I asked of his friends when they told me the sad news. "He has to have a birth name."

"Peter Fiah," was their reply.

In my head I replayed the first words Peter had ever spoken to me: "Hey my man, white man, my good friend I beg you please hear me-o."

I had heard him, with an unmistakable clarity.

*****

Coincidentally, just as Clarisa and I were preparing to leave Liberia, so was our friend Monsignor Karnley. The good priest's work had been noticed and the Vatican honored him with an offer of a three-year sabbatical to study in Rome. At the time Clarisa and I, though overjoyed for the monsignor, felt his absence from Liberia would be a loss. As it turned out, his stay in Italy was cut short when, in February 2011, Pope Benedict XVI appointed him the Bishop of Cape Palmas, in Maryland County. Our courageous friend, now Bishop Andrew Karnley, is back where he belongs and we couldn't be happier for him.

The last day was the hardest. For weeks, in an effort to soften our departure, we had been telling the boys and girls that our leaving was not the end but just the beginning of our beautiful relationship. But as the clock ticked down the hours closer to our departure this promise was less of a comfort to me; I saw it as more wishful thinking than true possibility. Clarisa was the stronger one – she kept us moving forward making sure that tasks were completed so that we would be ready when the time came for us to go. Still, we were both struggling with the goodbyes. We tried to keep sentimentality to a minimum so we busied ourselves with giving away clothes, knickknacks, and other items that we could not carry home in our suitcases. A steady stream of visitors came by the mission to bid us God's speed and farewell.

This was July and school was out; more than half of our children were away visiting relatives, though a core of 50 having no true homes beyond Liberia Mission remained. Clarisa and I spent as much time as we could with each child. The hugs were a bit longer; they were definitely stronger. I felt enveloped in love. We posed for a few final group pictures, and then it was time to leave. Pa Alfred waited behind the wheel of our truck. Clarisa and I loaded our suitcases and climbed in, waving goodbye to the children and mission staff. I noticed a number of long faces in the crowd, some wiped away tears.

Pa, who had always been so ready with a smile and a story sat stone-faced. "Still don't know why you feel you and Clarisa have to depart from us," he said.

I slapped his knee and tried to mask my own sadness, "Pa, have to teach the white people about palm butter and groundhog." I teased, referring to a Liberian delicacy I'd grown to like.

Pa's lips turned up just the slightest bit at the corners. I knew he would forgive our leaving in time.

On the ride to the airport I tried to memorize the countryside with its rubber plants and palm trees. I knew we were seeing these familiar sights for the last time. When we passed the road that led to Elijah Koko's grave, the tear that had been threatening finally spilled softly down my cheek. I said a prayer for my young friend.

As our plane took off from Roberts International Airport, I looked down at Liberia and accepted that I had been wrong about the country. It wasn't the wasteland I had first thought it was when we landed that dark night in September of 2008. I had learned so much in less than two years. I came as a teacher, but I was leaving as a student.

Over 350 lives – orphans, students, teachers, mission workers – touched mine and I touched theirs. We had become family. Clarisa and I had *felt* the rain, not just gotten wet. It had cleansed us.

I settled into my seat as Liberia disappeared from sight. Our plane climbed higher and we were soon engulfed by cotton candy clouds. This was the shortest leg of the journey, a two-hour flight to Accra, Ghana, and then a short layover before we made our way to Brussels, Belgium and finally Houston, Texas, U.S.A.

I kept thinking back to the kids, Pa Alfred, Mama Helena, Harris Mulbah, and all the others. My final thought before drifting off to sleep was of Musu. She was smiling.

Clarisa had been right all along, Liberia was worth it.

Epilogue: The Voice Was Love

**"Yesterday is gone. Tomorrow has not yet come.
We have only today. Let us begin."**
- Mother Teresa

I have never put too much stock in people who say they hear the voice of God. Often the outcome of such a claim is disastrous. Jim Jones and the tragedy that befell over 900 members of the Peoples Temple in Guyana in 1978 as well as the deaths of David Koresh and his Branch Davidians in Waco, Texas in 1993 are prime examples of what can go wrong when false prophets claim to hear God speak.

So what was I to make of my experience the morning of March 16, 2003 when I heard the voice? My first reaction was to think I had finally cracked and spun off into a dark void of psychosis, either that or I was suffering the consequences of a hangover after another night of excessive partying. I had been through a painful divorce and was fairly miserable most of the time. I was also mad at God and took my anger to its logical conclusion by abandoning my relationship with Him. For the longest time, if you asked me, I would say all I really wanted was some peace in my life. I just had no idea how to go about finding it.

Then, one morning while I was shaving I heard a very faint yet quite clear voice say to me: "Go back to the Mass."

Of course I wanted none of this nonsense so I ignored it. But, like a persistent itch, the voice came to me again and again, each time a little stronger, always saying the same thing, "Go back to the Mass."

On a Sunday morning, three weeks after the initial whisper in my ear, my mother woke me with an early morning call – a rarity for her – and I finally started to pay attention. My mother had been worried about the path I was on and though I was fighting the desire to hang up on her and crawl back under the comfort of my covers she stopped me with her words.

"If you are looking for peace, Jerome, I think you should start going back to Mass."

I knew right then that the voice had been real. It belonged to Christ who seemed to be, for whatever reason, in passionate pursuit of me. When I didn't respond to His voice, He made sure to speak through someone I loved and would be able to hear, my Mom.

After I hung up the receiver, I felt something akin to a seismic shift occur inside me. My sudden insight reinvigorated me so much that I decided to try and get over to the 7 a.m. Mass at my neighborhood church, St. Maximillian Kolbe. I hopped in the shower where I quickly began to backslide, trying to argue myself out of my hasty church-going decision. I was not quite ready to give up my old life without at least a little fight. I eventually lost the argument with myself and quickly dressed and headed out the door.

In my car on the way to church, I popped Jimi Hendrix and The Band of Gypsys into my CD player and tuned in a song I knew well,

"Message of Love." Suddenly I was struck by Hendrix's words like never before: "Well I'm traveling the speed of a reborn man. I got a lot of love to give from the mirrors of my hand." I was tapping the stick shift with my forefinger and thinking about the lyrics, "… traveling the speed of a reborn man, I got a lot of love to give …" Just like that with Hendrix, Billy Cox and Buddy Miles along for the ride I was on my way back to the Mass.

*****

As my Continental flight passed over the Gulf of Mexico, I was trying to figure out how I had arrived here. How, I asked myself, did a 37-year-old successful high school basketball coach with aspirations of reaching the college level, wind up on a flight to Tegucigalpa, Honduras to begin a new life as a missionary? That I had absolutely no understanding of Spanish beyond "hola" only made matters more curious.

My "back to Mass" odyssey led me to read more earnestly about spirituality. I started with Thomas A. Kempis' *Imitation of Christ* then moved on to *The Epistle of James* and an assortment of books written by and about Mother Teresa. Dorothy Day's *The Long Loneliness* impacted me greatly. I studied the discourses of Augustine, struggling through his *Confessions*. Reading the gospels made me feel like Jesus was my personal tutor. The closer I looked at the early Church and saints the more I was brought face to face with an obvious reality: It's not about me and never was. What my life was meant to be about was service to others.

I spent time studying my options and was ready to commit to the Peace Corps and a posting in Eastern Europe when I heard about Mission Honduras International, a Catholic organization serving the poor in Honduras. Here was an opportunity not just to serve others, I thought, but also to nourish my own spirit as well. So I headed south.

I finally slammed the door shut on my old life. I was ready; I felt alive and eager to make up for lost time. Honduras offered me a second chance and I would make the most of it.

The group of student volunteers from Loras College in Iowa was due to arrive in an hour at Toncontin International Airport in Tegucigalpa; I was their ride. At this point I had been in country about a year and a half. One of my duties as house director for volunteers visiting Mission Honduras was to shuttle volunteer groups to and from the airport and the mission site.

I calculated that I had at least an hour and a half probably two, before they cleared customs and were ready to make the hour and a half trip back to the mission's volunteer center in Comayagua. I headed across the street to kill time at Metro Media, just like I had a hundred times before. My intention was not unlike any other visit to the store, buy a few magazines and possibly a book while I waited for my incoming group of Americans. I liked Metro Media. It was clean, well-lit and trendy. It was a great place to relax before missionary groups came in. I knew the employees well and liked to practice my growing Spanish vocabulary with them.

The Loras College volunteers were the first to visit the mission in more than a month; as a result, I hadn't made any visits to the book store for quite some time. I was busy flipping through the information sheet provided to me via e-mail by the leader of the arriving group as I walked through the door and into the store.

I heard a friendly, but unfamiliar voice say, "Good morning sir, and welcome to Metro Media."

I lifted my head to respond – nothing in my life would ever be the same again.

I was greeted by a smile as big and bright as the sun topped by the most beautiful pair of eyes I had ever seen. My knees buckled as I had an anguished thought, "Oh my God, why can't I be in my twenties again?"

Blurting out a choked, "Fine, thank you. How are you?" I made a bee-line for the magazines where I sat down, winded, and wondered who was driving the truck that just ran me over.

I bought a ridiculous amount of magazines; some like *Redbook, Small Business Opportunities,* and *Car and Driver,* I had no intention of ever reading. I plopped the magazines down on the counter as I smiled and said, "Hola como esta?" We made small talk in Spanish. I bumbled along exposing my limited vocabulary, all the while trying not to let on just how flustered I was by the girl's breathtaking beauty.

When she finished totaling the magazines she said, "That will be $32.50 please," in perfect English. I happily switched to my native tongue, too, and our conversation grew easier.

The young woman asked me what I was doing in Honduras and when I explained that I was a Catholic missionary her interest peaked and she confided that she wanted to be a missionary in Africa when she graduated from college.

"Africa?" I asked. "We have a mission in Africa; it's in Liberia. I'm sure I could put you in touch with some people if you are serious."

While our organization did indeed have a mission in Liberia, I had absolutely no desire to go there.

Leaving the store I headed in the direction of the airport, pleased I had ventured into Metro Media. I had almost reached the freeway that divided the airport from the strip mall where Metro Media was located when I heard a voice call out, "Sir, sir, stop; please stop!"

I felt I must have made quite an impression on the young lady because she was chasing after me.

"You forgot your magazines," she said handing me a bag. I felt like an idiot.

"By the way my name is Jerome," I managed to squeeze out as I tried not to faint from embarrassment.

She smiled that sunny smile and said, "Nice to meet you Jerome; my name is Clarisa."

Clarisa and I eventually started dating. I couldn't believe how lucky I was, and even though there was seventeen years difference between us it didn't matter. Our relationship just worked, as a matter of fact, more easily that I could ever have anticipated. I fell deeply in love with Clarisa. She was surrounded by the light of Christ and this challenged me to be a better person and a better Catholic. That she loved me back allowed me to realize that I had found the greatest blessing I would ever receive in my life.

We were married at Santo Domingo Savio Catholic Church in Tegucigalpa on June 14, 2008. I trembled just a little when I saw Clarisa walk through the church door. She was radiant in her wedding dress, with her father at her side she came forward step by step closer to where I was waiting at the altar. In just a moment she would be my wife. The church was full of family and friends from Honduras as well as the United States; they were so happy for us.

My life had come full circle. By listening to that small quiet voice five years earlier I had begun a quest that led to this very moment. As we turned to face the priest to exchange our vows, a thought pushed its way into my head: What if I had never listened to the voice? What if I had never come to Honduras?

It made me shudder.

I came to realize that God was speaking to me all the time in many ways. So when Clarisa asked, once again, if we could go to Africa and do mission work, I finally heard her. Two months after our marriage we were on our way to Liberia.

Afterword

To understand the circumstances that sentenced the young men I introduced in "Little Generals" (as well as hundreds of others) to the streets of Monrovia we must go back to long before they were born.

For the first 133 years of its history Liberia was ruled and governed exclusively by Americo-Liberians and their True Whig Party. Americo-Liberian was the name given by the indigenous tribes to the freed slaves from the United States and their descendants who had repatriated to Africa and founded the Commonwealth of Liberia in 1822.

Throughout the history of the country, which declared itself a republic in 1845, the Americo- Liberians steadfastly remained the educated, the privileged and the elite of Liberian society. Although never comprising more than three and a half percent of the country's population, the Americo-Liberians controlled all aspects of the republic, including its wealth. Ironically the indigenous people were subjected to the same sub-human treatment by the Americo-Liberians that they themselves had faced at the hands of their overseers in the United States. The native tribes lived meager lives with little hope of rising out of the poverty in which they toiled. As they tired of token positions in society, business, and government, the seeds of discontent began to grow, silently, just under the surface for several generations. It was only a matter of time before revolution broke its way through the fertile soil of the Liberian landscape.

In April of 1980 the grip of the Americo-Liberians was finally shattered as the country they built came crashing down around them. Everything changed in the blink of an eye with the successful coup led by a meagerly educated Master Sergeant in the AFL (Armed Forces of Liberia) named Samuel Kanyon Doe. Doe represented hope for all indigenous Liberians as he was of the Krahn tribe from Grand Geddah County in eastern Liberia.

What Doe lacked in formal education, which stopped at the eighth grade, he more than made up for in audacity and determination. Leading a group of seventeen AFL soldiers under the name The People's Redemption Council, Doe stormed the Executive Mansion in the early morning hours of April 14th and assassinated elected President William Richard Tolbert. The daring and bloody raid effectively erased the power that the Americo-Liberians had firmly held over the country. Doe ascended to the presidency amid widespread jubilation from the indigenous tribes, which made up more than ninety percent of Liberia's population. Finally, a "man of the soil," as Samuel K. Doe was hailed, had become president.

The results of Doe's ascension to the presidency proved to be disastrous. He was a total failure and in time became more corrupt and bloodthirsty than any of the presidents who had served before him. Doe's power shift dissolved any unity that existed within the borders of Liberia and catapulted the country into tumult. What transpired over the next ten years ranged from embezzlement and stolen elections, to monstrous ethnic cleansing, murder, and cannibalism. Doe's strong-armed tactics and dictatorial methods set the stage for the entry of one of modern history's most infamous warlords Charles Ghanky Taylor.

Like Doe, Taylor was an indigenous native whose mother was a member of the Gola tribe. The most glaring difference between the two men was that while Doe was nearly illiterate and took what he wanted by force, Taylor was well educated having graduated from Bentley College in Waltham, Massachusetts in the U.S. Taylor was able to inspire devotion through his verbal persuasive power.

Set on overthrowing Doe and claiming executive power for himself Taylor started his own revolution on Christmas Eve 1989. Taylor, supported by the governments of the Ivory Coast, Sierra Leone, Burkina-Faso, and to a more clandestine degree, The United States, relentlessly pursued Doe and his followers. Taylor's rebel front was dubbed the NPFL (National Patriotic Front of Liberia).

In September 1990, ten years after seizing power, Doe was apprehended in a fire-fight at the Freeport of Monrovia. He was tortured and finally executed by his captors. In the end it wasn't Taylor who had cornered Doe and eliminated him, but another warlord (and Taylor's one time ally) Prince Yormie Johnson. Johnson had broken away from Taylor right before the Christmas Eve invasion and formed his own group of rebel combatants named the INPFL (Independent National Patriotic Front of Liberia).

Embarrassed by his lack of military success in his attempts to overthrow Doe, Taylor and his NPFL embarked on a spree of murder and mayhem. The country spiraled even more out of control as innocent Liberians suffered unspeakable degradations and death. Now it became impossible for ordinary civilians to determine who was friend or foe as many people were eager for their own share of success in the midst of chaos.

The removal of Doe did nothing to unify the country and civil war raged.

Liberia became more destabilized and chaotic than at any point in its previous history. Interim after interim president was put into power by international organizations to no avail. Throughout the early and mid-1990's Taylor launched military operations against the capital city of Monrovia. Tens of thousands died. Taylor and his NPFL controlled ninety percent of the country but his inability to take Monrovia kept him from achieving his ultimate goal of becoming president of the republic.

A series of peace accords drawn up by West African leaders and ever increasing scrutiny by an international audience brought a fragile but much needed respite from war. In 1997 Liberia held its first free presidential elections in more than a decade. The field of candidates was immense, twenty three in all. In the field of those vying to become president of Liberia was the charismatic Charles Taylor. In a single afternoon he was able to achieve what had been impossible for him to do in eight years of fighting; he took hold of the presidency of Liberia. He did it without firing a single shot.

Many Liberians believe Taylor was elected president because the populace feared he would return to war if he was denied the political victory. Held captive by fear, some Liberians even wore t-shirts bearing Taylor's image that ominously stated, "He Killed My Ma, He Killed My Pa – But I Will Vote for Him." Even so, most Liberians were cautiously optimistic about their future. Sadly all the future held for them was more corruption, war, and death. It seemed as though evil had taken up permanent residence in Liberia.

Rebel factions rose up in all parts of Liberia focused on removing Taylor form power. The two main bodies were the (LURD) Liberians

United for Reconciliation and Democracy and (MODEL) Movement for Democracy in Liberia. Although surrounded by a maelstrom, Taylor casually went about his unholy business. He supplied weapons to Sierra Leonean rebels who were fighting their own civil war in return for "blood" diamonds, timber, and ore. Through it all Taylor refused to acknowledge the precariousness of his own situation.

By 2003 Taylor, like Doe before him, had lost control of the country and now held only Monrovia. Under increasing international pressure from the United States, ECOWAS (Economic Community of West African States) and The United Nations, Taylor stepped down from power in August of 2003 after being granted asylum in Nigeria. Liberia no longer resembled a country. What Taylor left behind was an apocalyptic wasteland. The civil conflicts that had raged for more than 20 years took the lives of more than 250,000 of its citizens. As of this writing Charles Taylor is being tried by the UN's International Criminal Court in The Hague, Netherlands for his crimes against humanity.

Sadly his popularity in Liberia is still strong among certain groups of people, namely the elite as well of those he had deceived into believing he was an upright man.

When asked if he would still be well received in Liberia if he were somehow able to return I was greeted with the response by an elderly man, "The red carpet would begin in The Hague and end in Monrovia."

The wars are still fresh in the minds of those who lived through them. The old adage that "time heals all wounds" doesn't bring much comfort for those still struggling to survive in the here and now.

I spoke to an Americo-Liberian woman at Roberts International Airport in 2009, six full years after the second civil war had ground to a halt. Here is what she told me: "They destroyed the entire nation. Other countries, like Sierra Leone, Mozambique or Rwanda at least left an infrastructure. They had a specific point when the wars ended in their countries. The ability to rebuild was taken away from us by these crazy people. Look around at what you have seen, how long do you think it will take to build something significant here, if ever? I am waiting on a plane to carry me to Ghana. Can you believe that? Ghanaians used to come to us, to Liberia, but now we Liberians go anywhere to get out of our own country. They killed our mothers and fathers and worse of all they killed our children. Our country is a joke to the rest of the world."

Throughout the civil conflicts that plagued Liberia the children, some as young as eight, were seen as an expendable commodity. Charles Taylor used thousands of children during his invasion of Liberia in 1989 and again in its defense as rebels closed in around him in 2003. Sadly the use of child soldiers wasn't relegated only to Charles Taylor. The ranks of rebel factions that roamed the hills and grasslands of Liberia were also swollen by child soldiers.

Liberia became a killing field where babies killed babies.

Meeting some of those former child soldiers years later on the streets of Monrovia I saw that they were living hopeless lives; begging to survive with permanently mutilated bodies. It made me question if their survival had been a blessing or a curse. That is the enduring tragedy of Liberia.

As I write this the civil wars have been over for almost eight years, yet Liberia still struggles for survival. The country's plight is reflected in statistics that portray an austere existence. Depending on who is doing the counting, the numbers differ slightly, it is generally agreed that Liberia suffers rates of 80 percent unemployment and 75 percent illiteracy. Males can expect to live an average of 44.7 years, females a bit longer at 47.3 years. Seventy percent of the country is between the ages of 18-35 and more than 60 percent of these young adults are without work or education. Those lucky enough to have jobs take home around 100 L.D. (Liberian Dollars) a day, the equivalent of $1.42 U.S.

Malaria, typhoid, and pneumonia are constant unwanted companions of the Liberian populace. Sadly diabetes has become more prevalent as well. Even with an abundance of religious and secular aid organizations offering assistance a severe shortage of medical professionals persists in the country, with less than 0.5 doctors for every 1,000 Liberians.

Yet, in the face of the kind of despair these statistics engender, there is actual cause for hope. Though Samuel Doe and Charles Taylor destroyed a country, they did not succeed in destroying the spirit of its people. I have seen firsthand their resilience. I have seen them praise God for the chance at another day of life. Even when they were abandoned by civilized society, pitied but not helped, they somehow found the will to carry on.

The devil had walked Liberia through the gates of hell then abandoned her expecting that she would be too defeated to turn around and find her way out again. But the devil celebrated prematurely. Today Liberia is on the mend, and though it is no panacea, it is a far cry from the hopeless, abandoned nation of the late 20th century. This is due in large part to renewed government leadership especially that of Madam Helen Johnson-Sirleaf, the first woman to be elected to the presidency of an African country.

The task that she inherited upon her election in 2005 was daunting to say the least. What lay in front of her was devastation. I have often compared President Johnson-Sirleaf's situation with that of a firefighter standing in front of an inferno armed only with a squirt gun.

Her administration has invested greatly in rebuilding national pride and the educational system within Liberia. Her efforts have been hampered by corruption in her own government and the constant struggle against the common enemies of illiteracy, inadequate health care, and poverty. Although there is much work to be done, Clarisa and I saw marked improvements in our two years there.

Liberia is a country of young people so it falls to them to continue the fight to improve their country's place in the world: But instead of guns they must learn to wield pencils and instead of blades they must do battle with their books if they are to achieve anything lasting. They have already learned through experience the futility of war, now they must arm themselves with knowledge. Even so, before Liberia can ever hope to regain a place of prominence among nations it will have a very long and hard road to traverse, every step of the way fraught with disease, poverty, and ignorance tempting it to despair.

I probably will never see Liberia's rise. But perhaps some of the children that Clarisa and I grew to know and love at Liberia Mission will live to see it. Perhaps a few will even play important parts in their country's resurgence by becoming doctors, teachers, and business leaders – maybe even president of the republic.

For the small part I have been allowed to play in the Liberian story I am grateful. For the very large part my Liberian friends have played in restoring my sense of purpose I will never be able to adequately express my gratitude. I thank God every day I was able to leave a footprint or two along Liberia's path to recovery.

Acknowledgements

Many great people have made this book a reality. I would like to thank first and foremost Jesus Christ for blessing me more than I deserve. All praise and glory to the King of Kings. I could write a book about Clarisa but for now I love you, you are my hero and my strength. Barbara Pawlikowski took a jumbled mess of ideas and helped me shape and develop it. I am honored beyond words to have her associated with this project. Her belief in me and her encouragement is what got me over the top. John and Sue Dewan have been heroes in many people's lives for so long, now Liberia has felt their love and it's a better country for it. Bob O'Dwyer along with John fought every day for truth, justice and peace. They kept us afloat in Liberia physically and spiritually. I love you. Joanie Fabiano, Cathy O'Dwyer, Steve Hayes, Monica Desmond and Todd Looby, Tom Teeling , Ed and Jennie Martin, and Dave Dionisi – being able to call you friends is the greatest blessing in my life.

A special debt of gratitude to the Bishop of Cape Palmas, Liberia Andrew Karnley, Matt Hayes, Father Don Halpin and Father John Stowe who battled on the front lines with me and Clarisa in Liberia. This book doesn't exist without you.

For Paul Devore who knows me better than I know myself. This book was brought to you by the letter "L". The only thing that matters is if the love remains. I love you "Devo".

To my brothers Jules Jr., Jay, Jimmy and Jon, my father Jules Peyton Cabeen Sr. and my mother Joan Cabeen. I love you with all my heart.

For Betty Grissom and Yvonne Noggle who hold a big place in my heart. We served together in Honduras for four years and Yvonne almost gave her life while on mission in Liberia. I love the both of you more than you'll ever know.

Para mis queridos suegros Renato y Ethel Chavarria. Los quiero por darme Clarisa y dejarme ser parte de su familia. (To my beautiful in-laws—I love you for giving me Clarisa and letting me be part of your family.)

A sincere debt of gratitude to the good people of West Africa, especially those in Liberia, who struggle everyday for survival. Your love and hospitality to Clarisa and I will forever be remembered. Keep the faith!

And finally to all the beautiful children I was blessed to serve and live with in Honduras and Liberia. You have saved my soul.

- Jerome Cabeen

References

Beah, Ishmael. *A Long Way Gone: Memoirs of a Boy Soldier.* New York: Sarah Crichton Books (Farrar, Straus and Giroux), 2007.

Guannu, Joseph Saye. *Liberian History Up To 1847* (Third Edition), Monrovia: Sabanoh Printing Press Ltd, 1997.

Johnson, Prince Yormie. *The Rise and Fall of Samuel K. Doe – A Time To Heal and Rebuild Liberia.* Lagos: Pax Cornwell Publishers Ltd., 1991.

McKissack, Patricia C. & Fredrick L. *Rebels Against Slavery.* New York: Scholastic Incorporated, 1996.

Reef, Catherine. *This Our Dark Country: The American Settlers of Liberia.* New York: Houghton Mifflin. 2002.

Republic of Liberia. *Agenda – Truth and Reconciliation Commission Final Report. Volume III: Appendices –Title II: Children, the Conflict and the TRC Children.* Monrovia: Republic of Liberia, 2009.

Sleh, Aaron C., Toe, Samuel G., Weah, Aaron B. *Impunity Under Attack-The Evolution and Imperatives of The Liberian Truth Commission.* Monrovia: Civic Initiative, 2008.

Tolbert, Victoria Anna David. *Lifted Up. Minneapolis:* Macalester Park, 1996.

For more information on **<u>Liberia Mission Incorporated</u>** please visit:

www.missionhonduras.com

www.liberiamission.org

www.facebook.com/pages/Liberia-Mission-Inc

Visit **"Memoirs of a Reluctant Servant"** on:

www.facebook.com/pages/Memoirs-of-a-Reluctant-Servant

&

www.readreluctantservant.com